STREET SMART FRANCHISING

STREET SMART FRANCHISING

JOE MATHEWS, DON DEBOLT
AND DEB PERCIVAL
THE FRANCHISE PERFORMANCE GROUP

EP Entrepreneur® Press

Editorial Director: Jere Calmes
Cover Design: Todd Sumney
Editorial and Production Services: CWL Publishing Enterprises, Inc.,
  Madison, Wisconsin, www.cwlpub.com

This publication is designed to provide accurate and authoritative information in regard to the subject matter covered. It is sold with the understanding that the publisher is not engaged in rendering legal, accounting,
or other professional services. If legal advice or other expert assistance is
required, the services of a competent professional person should be
sought.

—From a Declaration of Principles jointly adopted by
a Committee of the American Bar Association and
a Committee of Publishers and Associations

ISBN 1-59918-021-9

Library of Congress Cataloging-in-Publication Data
Mathews, Joe.
    Street Smart franchising : read this before you buy a franchise! / by
Joe Mathews, Don DeBolt, and Deb Percival.
        p. cm.
    ISBN 1-59918-021-9 (alk. paper)
    1. Franchises (Retail trade) I. DeBolt, Don. II. Percival, Deb.
III. Title.
HF5429.23.M38 2006
658.8'708--dc22

                                                2006013791

10 09 08   10 9 8 7 6 5 4

Printed in Canada

Contents

**Part One. What You Need to Know Before
You Start Looking** **1**

Chapter 1. What's a Franchise? 3
Franchise /franchiz/ 3
Franchising as a Distribution Model 3
A Better Definition—Franchising as a Relationship 4
Franchising as a Strategy to Co-create a Desired Future 5
Franchising as a Calling 5
The Best Definition—Franchising as One Body 6
Why People Invest in Franchises 7
Why Do Companies Franchise? 8
Spotting a High Road Franchisor 11
Recruiting Top-Quality Franchise Candidates 14
Developing Peak-Performing Franchisees 17
Building a Strong Franchisee Community 19

Chapter 2. Why Should I Invest in a Franchise? 22
The Path of the 99 Percent 23
The Path of the 1 Percent 24
The Voice of the Inner Critic 25
The "Right" Business 27
The "Right Time" to Start a Business 28

Contents

The Differences Between the 1 Percent and
  the 99 Percent   29
How to Join the 1 Percent   30
Creating a Desired Future   31

Chapter 3. Understanding Your Behavior Style   34
Behavior Styles   34
How Does DISC Work?   39
You Are an Action Hero If ...   39
You Are a Comedian If ...   45
You Are a Faithful Sidekick If ...   48
You Are a Private Eye If ...   51
What Character Do You Play?   55
How Can I Predict Others' Styles?   57

Chapter 4. What Does Winning Look Like?   59
Goal Setting and Benchmarks   60
Goals Schmoals! Why Should I Care About Goals?   63
Making Your Desired Future S.M.A.R.T.   65
S.M.A.R.T. Goals   65
How Do You Eat an Elephant?   67
The Seven Truths About Real Time   69
How Do You Get This Information?   76

**Chapter 5. What Does It Take to Win
as a Franchisee?   83**
The KASH Model of Success   87
The Costs of Poor Performance   91
The KASH Deficit Analysis   92
What Is Your Starting KASH Balance?   96

Chapter 6. The Learning Curve of a Franchisee   98
Three Modes of Franchisor KASH Distribution   100
The Launch   107
Strategies for a Successful Launch   110
The Grind   111
Strategies to Successfully Navigate the Grind   121
How the Franchisor Can Help You Navigate the Grind   123
Winning   124

Contents

Strategies for Successfully Navigating from Winning
   to the Zone 128
How the Franchisor Can Help You Win? 129
The Zone 130
How the Franchisor Can Help You in the Zone 132
The Goodbye 133
How the Franchisor Can Help You with the Goodbye 138

**Chapter 7. The Evolution of the Franchisee-
Franchisor Relationship 140**
The Glee Stage 142
The Fee Stage 144
The Me Stage 146
The Free Stage 147
The See Stage 149
The We Stage 151
From Glee to We 152

Part Two. Investigating Franchises 155

Chapter 8. Locating Franchise Opportunities 157
Franchise Opportunity Web Sites 158
Franchise Brokers 159
Magazines 160
Franchise Expos 160
Newspapers 160

**Chapter 9. Following a Six-Step Franchise
Investigation Process 161**
Overview of the Six-Step Franchise
   Investigation Process 164
Step One: The Initial Interview 167
Step Two: Qualification 174
Step Three: Reviewing the UFOC and
   Franchise Agreements 179
Step Four: Franchisee Validation, Data Gathering,
   and Analysis 195
Step Five: Attending a Discovery Day or Visiting
   the Home Office 207
Franchise Cultures 209

Contents

Decision-Making Checklist   217
Step Six: Making an Investment Decision   220
Final Decision Worksheet   223
Conclusion   223

Index   **227**

Introduction

Your Purpose—Our Purpose

If you're reading this you're probably looking for a way to create a great, happy, powerful, productive life for you and your family. Perhaps the track you're on now, which was fine to get you where you are, just isn't going to take you where you want to go next. Some people will get a bit frustrated and discouraged, mourning their past. Others are pumped up, excited about the changes that lie ahead. Still others are simply afraid, lost in the ambiguity of what will happen next. Regardless of where you are or what you're experiencing, if you think you might be interested in franchising, this book was written for you.

The purpose *of Street Smart Franchising* is to prep you about what it takes to succeed in franchising, walk you to the starting line of owning a franchise, show you the finish line of peak productivity and personal success, and give you a proven strategy on how to win the race.

Franchising has opened worlds of possibilities for hundreds of thousands of people. According to a recent study commissioned by The International Franchise Association, there are approximately 770,000 franchised outlets representing more than 70 different industries in the United States alone. A recent study by PriceWaterhouse-Coopers stated that franchising generates nearly 10 percent of the economy of the entire U.S. private sector.. Furthermore, franchising accounts for almost 14 percent of job creation. In another study, more than 90 percent of franchisees indicated they considered themselves successful. Simply put, franchising works and people just like you are winning.

Franchising, while wildly successful, simply isn't for everyone. Starting a business is a lonely and emotionally taxing undertaking, and is not for the weak of heart. Starting any business is an emotional rollercoaster. Right now, you're in the lead car of the rollercoaster, slowly clicking your way to the top of that first steep hill. You can see the drop, but you can't see past it. The anticipation of what happens next makes the ride both frightful and exciting. At the end of the wild ride, as you contemplate the wind in your hair, the speed of the coaster, and the twists of the track, chances are you will be happy you bought the ticket.

It's estimated that more than one million people each year (mostly employees) investigate starting a franchise. Conversely, relatively few existing franchise owners leave self-employment to look for jobs. Be careful; once you take on the identity of "entrepreneur," you may never want to take it off again. Being an entrepreneur won't describe what you do, it will describe who you are. While the personal transformation from employee to entrepreneur may be uncomfortable, it is liberating. Few ever reverse the process. We've heard it best described in two ways. First, "Once a pickle, never a cucumber again," and "Once the genie is out of the bottle, you can't get him back in."

Franchising is a terrific avenue for people who want to work *for* themselves but not *by* themselves. Franchising offers entrepreneurs both business and emotional support during trying times. Franchisors' proven business models, tools for success, and ongoing support are invaluable.

If you're a normal human being, you're thrilled by the possibilities—and petrified of the unknown. You may say to yourself, "I don't understand franchising. It's intimidating. How will I pick the right one? What will happen to me and my family if I fail?"

That's where we come in. We have bought franchises, sold franchises, trained franchisees (people like you who have invested in a franchise), coached franchisors (companies who license their business systems to franchisees), supplied franchisors and franchisees, and held leadership roles in the industry's premier organizations. We've seen every side of the business. No other franchising book that we know of covers the depth of material we'll give you here.

We wrote this book to guide you through the process of investigating a franchise and to serve as a handbook for years to come.

We'll give you the tools to create a customized launch pad *and* a personal plan for success. If you already have a plan for success, this book will help you develop a better, more informed one.

You've already heard that franchising is not for everyone. As a matter of fact, franchisors report that out of 100 people who request information about starting a business, *only one percent* actually join the franchise.

You may ask yourself, "If franchising is so successful (and it is), and a vast majority of franchisees succeed (and they do), why do only one percent of the people invest in a franchise?"

That's a very logical question. But consider that logic has little to do with it. Most people don't make logical decisions, they make emotional ones. The emotional decision is almost always "no." But most of the 99 percent who investigate starting a franchise start with "no" and then find reasons to say "yes." Regardless of the franchise, you can always find a reason to say "no."

For instance, how would you like to own a business with extremely high employee turnover, high overhead, high lease costs, high equipment costs, low margins, and high advertising costs? The average customer will only spend a few dollars, so you're forced to do hundreds of transactions a day, just to keep the lights on. You have to move customers through your business at such a feverish pace, you can't provide much in the way of customer service. As a matter of fact, extended customer interactions make the business model break down. You've got to keep your customers moving in and out. Speed is the key. And your business is completely dependent on minimum-wage workers. Because employee turnover is so high, you're always on the lookout for additional minimum-wage workers. Sometimes you will keep more people on the payroll than you really need because you know that some people are going to quit. Other times, you're left understaffed and have to hire the first breathing human who walks through the door. Would you ever want to own a business like that?

If you answered "no" to owning this business, you just rejected McDonald's®.

Now, let's rephrase the question. Assuming you had the necessary capital, met their stringent qualifications, and the opportunity existed for you, how would you like to own a McDonald's® restaurant? Did your answer change?

Every business has its own share of problems. When you invest in a franchise, you are investing in proven solutions to everyday business challenges. For instance, McDonald's® has processes and systems in place that make high employee turnover manageable.

With a healthy dose of self-awareness, the proper preparation, the ability to pick not only a good franchise but the right one for you, and knowledge of how to be an effective franchise owner, your chances of success increase exponentially. And that's an increase over the already tremendous success ratio that franchising enjoys.

Whether your dream is to make more money, have multiple streams of income, have more control, spend time with your family, travel, retire early, or leave a legacy for your family, franchising can help you get there.

This book will:

- Help you decide if franchising is for you.
- Tell you what you will see, feel, and experience before you invest.
- Help you manage your emotions and perceptions throughout the investigation process.
- Help you determine what type of franchise—with your specific skills, talents, and short-comings—you can have the greatest success in.
- Show you how to accelerate your learning curve, to achieve peak performance.
- Give you the real world tactics and strategies so you can develop your own comprehensive plan for success.

Perhaps most important, you will have a road map to help you act from a place of logic rather than fear.

Street Smart Franchising is broken down into two parts. Part One, the first seven chapters, gives you an insider's look at what it takes to win in franchising. While most books on franchising discuss the topic from an academic perspective, we show you how franchising *really works from an inside, real world perspective.* Among other things:

- We will show you exactly what competent and incompetent franchisors look like and detail for you the telltale signs and indicators.
- We will tell you exactly what franchising is and isn't, addressing common misperceptions.
- You will identify the style you use to naturally produce

results, learning what will and won't work in franchising.

- You will discover the obstacles and barriers you may put in your own way, limiting your success and stealing your own dreams.
- You will understand exactly what you can and cannot count on a franchisor for and what a franchisor will count on you to do.

When you complete Part One, you will have a clear vision for what to look for in a franchise and what to avoid, what works and what doesn't.

In Part Two, we will take you through an intelligent, six-step process that will help you identify whether or not a particular franchise you're investigating fits who you are, delivers what you're looking to achieve with a high degree of probability, is run by a competent franchisor, and is built to last.

When you turn the final page you will be ready to make a decision. This isn't a book that will leave you thinking, "Maybe someday...."

Do you want this book to do these things for you? If so, you need to go through it from beginning to end, chapter by chapter. Don't skip around or the work will lose its impact. In franchising it's critical to be able to follow a proven process; one that's designed by someone else for your benefit, from start to finish. If you find yourself jumping around in this book after we've already informed you about the importance of following the process, the value of this work is diminished. Use this as an indicator for determining whether or not franchising is right for you.

If you're reading this book you are also probably a dreamer. You catch yourself thinking about what it's like to own a business. You think about your customers, who they are and what they will be like. You think about the difference your business will make to your customers, your employees, your family, and the community at large.

But what is your timeframe for making this happen? What is your plan?

Perhaps you have hope but no committed plan. While hope is nice, it's a lousy plan. You need a focused plan.

After reading *Street Smart Franchising*, your plans may take you in a direction, away from franchising and entrepreneurship, but you will have done so from a place of knowledge and real world experience, rather than moving away from fear, driven by false information and misperceptions. It will give you freedom and acceptance for your next career or the one you already have.

Whatever you do, it's ultimately your decision. And it's our commitment to you that your decision brings you freedom and peace.

Acknowledgments

For their help on this book I would like to specifically thank Jere Calmes and Leanne Harvey of Entrepreneur Press. Matthew Shay, President, Doc Cohen, Chairman, Debra Moss, and Anne Poodiack of the International Franchise Association (IFA). John Reynolds, President, Steve Greenbaum, Chairman, and Rose Dupont of the Institute of Certified Franchise Executives. Fred Deluca, founder of Subway and Jim Hansen, CEO of The National Association of Subway Franchisees. Also thanks to John Woods, CWL Publishing, Todd Sumney, Steve Schick, Bruce Krebs, Frank Morrison, Gus Iurillo, Harry Lew, Lynn Giulianni, Greg Nathan, Bob Lewis, Mary Ellen Sheets, Ken Bowen, Frank Fiume, Chris Brown, Paul Hogan, and Chuck Jones, Mary Mathews, and Dan Wilson.

About the Franchise Performance Group

The Franchise Performance Group is a street smart franchise consulting firm dedicated to helping franchisors win by helping them recruit, train, and develop peak performing franchisees.

Proven strategies for recruiting high quality franchisees. We train and develop franchisor's salespeople into high powered, high integrity, peak performing franchisee recruiters.

Proven strategies for ramping franchisees up faster. We help franchisors to assist franchisees to grasp the success formula of their business quicker, accelerating them through the learning curve towards peak performance.

Executive coaching for Franchisors and Franchisees. We offer one-on-one, results-oriented personal performance coaching for C-level executives and VP's of franchise companies, master licensees, area developers, and franchisees.

Contact Information
Phone: (860) 567-3099
Internet: www.franchiseperformancegroup.com

Part One

What You Need to Know Before You Start Looking

Chapter 1

What's a Franchise?

Franchise /franchiz/

According to Webster's Dictionary, a franchise is "the right or license granted to an individual or group to market a company's goods or services in a particular territory." The company offering the license is called "the franchisor"; the person investing in the license is called "the franchisee"; and the license is called "the franchise." Webster's defines franchising in terms of a legal business relationship. This is indeed an important aspect of franchising, but it doesn't tell the whole story.

Franchising as a Distribution Model

A popular book on franchising defines a franchise as "a system for expanding and distributing goods and services—and an opportunity to operate a business under a recognized brand name." Here franchising is described as both a distribution model for getting products and services to market and as a business opportunity. Franchisors rely on franchisees, which are independent businesspeople, to get the franchisor's products and services to market.

These are important aspects of franchising, but they don't capture the essence of what franchising really is or can be.

A Better Definition—Franchising as a Relationship

The relationship between franchisees (the independent businesspeople who license the franchisor's name and operating systems) and skilled franchisors (the parent company) transcend the boundaries of any existing legal and business relationships. Their relationships are highly personal. The franchisees and the franchisor, in their successful dealings with each other, form a tight-knit community. Franchising reduces itself to a business relationship only when these personal relationships either break down or were never properly cemented in the first place. Franchising further degenerates into a legal relationship only when business relationships are harmed. If franchisees and franchisors only define their relationship in terms of legal and business relationships, they aren't thinking big enough. Trust, respect, and open communication define these relationships.

The franchise relationship is grounded in a sacred trust and mutual respect between franchisees and franchisors. Each has a mission-critical job to do; each greatly jmpacts the other. Like combat soldiers in a platoon, franchisees and franchisors completely depend on each other to execute their jobs well to ensure mutual survival.

The franchisees' job is to serve their customers to the best of their ability consistent with the original intent of the franchisor. The franchisor's job is to maintain the integrity of the brand and create processes, systems, structures, products, marketing, and other resources which produce results that are far superior to any that one or two franchisees could produce for themselves.

Franchising as a Strategy to Co-create a Desired Future

Zig Ziglar once said, "People don't buy drills, they buy holes." Consider that people really don't invest in franchises, they really invest in some desired future consisting of both the financial and quality of life rewards associated with owning a business.

The International Franchise Association (IFA) estimates there are more than 2,000 franchisors representing more than 70 different industries. As you can see, there are a lot of different tools in the franchising toolbox, meaning thousands of potential outcomes. Any desired result anyone could ever want to achieve for themselves and their families is currently available in franchising.

Anyone who looks into investing in a franchise ultimately is faced with a decision. "Do I compromise on my dreams and stay on the path I already know, or do I take a chance and try to create the life I want?"

Currently there are more than 770,000 franchisee-owned outlets in the United States. Every franchisee has come to the exact same crossroads. Few who invest in a franchise are completely aware of everything it takes to succeed within that franchise. However, in the face of not knowing, they still take a bold step of faith and trust the franchisor with both their money and their dreams.

On the flip side, those who work for the franchisors also have dreams. They, too, want their lives and careers to look a particular way. They are counting on their franchisees to help them achieve their dreams. Each is co-creator of the other's future.

This trust transcends the terms of their franchise agreement.

Franchising as a Calling

To franchisees, the franchisor is their chosen vehicle to get them from where they are now to where they want to be. They are called to risk their lives, dreams, and resources to the care and talents of the franchisor who will assist them in creating their desired life.

For the franchisor, the franchisee is the chosen vehicle to take the franchisor from where they are now to where they want to be in the future. They risk their proprietary systems, products, and business secrets to the care of the franchisees.

Each is called forward into the service of the other.

As the founder and CEO of a youth sports franchise once said, "This franchise has ceased being a business to me. Youth sports is now what I'm called to do; it's bigger than me. I am blessed by surrounding myself with franchisees who experience the same calling."

The Best Definition—Franchising as One Body

Oddly enough, perhaps the best definition of franchising was written 2,000 years ago. As you read this, think of a franchise as one body consisting of several members: the franchisor (the parent company), franchisees (business owners), suppliers, and customers.

> The body does not consist of one member but of many. If the foot would say, "Because I am not a hand, I do not belong to the body," that would not make it any less a part of the body. And if the ear would say, "Because I am not an eye, I do not belong to the body," that would not make it any less a part of the body. If the whole body were an eye, where would the hearing be? If the whole body were hearing, where would the sense of smell be? ... If all were a single member, where would the body be? As it is, there are many members, yet one body. The eye cannot say to the hand, "I have no need of you," nor again the head to the feet, "I have no need of you." On the contrary, the members of the body that seem to be weaker are indispensable...But God has so arranged the body, giving the greater honor to the inferior member, that there may be no dissension within the body, but the members may have the same care for one another. If one member suffers, all suffer together with it; if one member is honored, all rejoice together with it.

While many franchisors may embrace this definition, not all do. The founder and CEO of a successful national franchise recently spoke at a national convention for franchise executives. During his presentation a member of the audience asked, "How do you resolve conflicts with your franchisees?"

He proudly threw back his shoulders and with his chest out proclaimed, "When push comes to shove, the franchisees know *this is my company!*"

Keep in mind, this company is currently very successful. However, his approach to franchising causes the pushing and shoving he spoke of. This approach to franchise leadership is the equivalent of the head saying to the feet, "When push comes to shove, *this is my body!*" And perhaps according to terms of the franchise agreement it is.

But someday, the head will need to walk someplace. That's when the head will have some issues.

As you investigate different franchises, find a franchisor whose leadership sees franchising as one body. If, in your search, you find a franchisor who thinks it's *their body*; where they are the head and the lowly franchisees are at the feet, seize the opportunity to be the feet … and run!

Why People Invest in Franchises

Remember, "People don't buy drills, they buy holes." The franchise is a drill. The most common reasons people report looking into franchising as a career option are:

- **More flexibility in their day.** Franchisees look for greater input in their day-to-day activities.
- **More control.** Franchisees want the authority and responsibility to make the decisions which impact their business and careers. They look to create a more performance-based and less political-based work life.
- **More work-life balance.** Many franchisees discovered that their past careers were consuming them, jeopardizing their closest personal relationships. Many start franchises as a way to spend more time with family, which may also include working with family members.
- **Greater personal challenge.** Many franchisees had either

reached the pinnacle of their professional careers or were competent to the point of no longer being challenged. They were in some version of a career rut and desperately needed a change.

- **Giving back to the community or making a difference in the lives of others.** Many franchisees have achieved financial stability or a measure of success in their past careers. They felt it was time to give something back.
- **Financial gain.** Many franchisees have a track record of success, creating wealth for shareholders or owners of other companies. It became time to create more equity and greater wealth for themselves and their families.

Shockingly, the least important of these reasons is financial gain. Most people report that if they could make a lateral move in earnings and still achieve the nonfinancial (quality of life) results they are looking for, they would make the jump into franchising. We will explore what both starts and stops people looking into franchising in much greater detail later in this book.

Why Do Companies Franchise?

There are two prevailing reasons why companies choose to franchise. The first we will call "the high road," and the second we will call "the low road."

The High Road to Franchising

Franchisors who take the high road possessed multiple options to expand their business. They had a proven business model which produced great results; including replicating their success in other markets. Some possible expansion strategies included bringing in investors, raising capital, and expanding through the chain method (where the parent company would own all the individual distribution points). Or they could restructure their companies and expand through franchising.

They chose franchising because franchising could provide them advantages that the chain method could not.

The first competitive advantage franchising can offer companies is stronger tactical execution of their business model by having entrepreneurs run point on the implementation rather than company managers. An entrepreneur with their dreams and money at stake will usually try harder and therefore produce greater results than an employee with only their bonus and job security at risk.

Second, franchising is a financing vehicle. Rather than having to raise millions of dollars to expand their business, franchisors leverage the franchisees' ability to raise capital through resources such as the Small Business Administration (SBA), home equity, and family.

Third, a franchise is typically better positioned to grow more quickly than a company that chooses the chain method of expansion. It was once said that "timing is everything." Good businesspeople know that when a market opportunity presents itself, it must be seized.

Fourth, franchising can be lower risk. Franchisors earn fees (royalties), which franchisees typically pay, from gross sales, not cash flow. Additionally, the start-up capital of the new business is the franchisees' risk, not the franchisor's. Although the franchisees assume much of the financial risk, the franchisor is dependent on the continuing royalty stream that franchisees pay. Additionally, franchisors won't grow if the franchisees aren't making money and achieving great results. Therefore, franchisors have a vested interest in helping the franchisees become profitable, but don't take the hit if they fail.

Fifth, they want to share their successes and make a difference in the lives of others. Most franchisors are deeply committed people who love to see their teammates win.

Lastly, franchisees have a collective genius that's hard to replicate using the chain method. For instance, a McDonald's® franchisee thought of the Big Mac.® Franchisees, not employees of the franchisor, are responsible for most of the breakthrough "million-dollar ideas" in a franchise organization.

The Low Road to Franchising

Many franchisors get into franchising because some consultant or attorney in a blue, pin-striped suit and a snappy red power tie told them that they could get rich using other people's money. And for only $75,000 they will show them how!

You can spot a "low road" franchisor by the following indicators:

- They are undercapitalized. Their company's financial survival is completely dependent on the short-term revenue from selling franchises instead of long-term revenue from collecting royalties. There appears to be no other source of expansion capital available. They have to sell you a franchise simply to survive.

- They haven't been in business more than five years or don't have a proven business model. They expect you to invest *your money for the privilege of proving* their business model for them.
- They have never expanded in multiple units and therefore haven't proven they can replicate their success. They are expecting you to jump at the opportunity to let them experiment with your money while their cash sits in their bank … assuming they have cash at all.
- Their unit economics don't provide them with a healthy enough return to expand by investing their own money. Yet somehow they believe it's good enough for you.

Not all "low road" franchisors are low-integrity people.

The founder of a fitness franchise was looking for assistance in recruiting franchisees. When the consultant reviewed the franchisor's financial statements, the consultant discovered that the franchisor had a corporate worth of $25 … no kidding, twenty-five bucks. Some people have lost more money in their sofa cushions than that franchisor had in his whole company. He was asked, "Does this financial statement accurately reflect your financial position or do you franchise under a shell corporation?" Keep in mind, many franchisors are private companies, and as such, their attorneys and accountants advise them not to keep large assets in their corporations. That's why many franchisors are actually stronger financially than they appear on paper.

However, this man responded, "That's all I have." Sadly, this good man was rejected as a client because he wasn't in a financial position to be able to support franchisees and grow his company.

This franchisor only had $25 because some consultant clipped him for about $60,000 to set him up as a franchisor. The founder had the noble intention of curbing the out-of-control obesity rate in America and promote active and healthy lifestyles. Unfortunately, this didn't happen. The road to hell is paved with good intentions.

Most franchise consultants and attorneys are respectable people and good at what they do. Just as there are a small number of franchisors who prey on the dreams and best intentions of gullible prospective franchisees, there are a small number of consultants and attorneys who prey on the dreams and best intentions of prospective franchisors. Both predators are a stain on franchising. Fortunately, both are in the minority.

Most franchisors are "high road" franchisors and some are "low road." Most "low road" franchisors are simply not going to make it. As you read on, you will learn how to distinguish one from the other.

Spotting a High Road Franchisor

What business are they in? While every franchisor distributes its own brand of products and services, *the franchise business model is a business unto itself.*

For example, Subway® restaurants are in the business of selling sandwiches. Thousands of restaurants, diners, and delis across the United States have made sandwiches a staple item on their menus. Any of these could have been Subway.® The difference was that Subway® founder Fred Deluca looked at a sandwich and saw opportunity, where others simply saw meat between two slices of bread.

Deluca knew, like McDonald's® mastermind Ray Kroc before him knew, it wasn't enough just to be brilliant at making sandwiches. Fred Deluca realized he not only had to be a brilliant restauranteur, but *he also had to become a brilliant franchisor.* Deluca saw that franchising was a business unto itself. As you investigate franchises, you will find that brilliant business models are a dime a dozen. However, *brilliant franchisors are few.* It takes a brilliant franchisor to build a strong regional or national brand.

If you were to ask CEOs of franchise companies, "What business are you in?" you will probably hear about the products and services they distribute, such as, "I'm in the auto repair business" or "I'm in the home furnishings business." You will seldom hear, "I'm in the franchising business."

Before investing your savings in a franchise, you may want to make sure you're doing business with a franchisor who understands *he's in the franchising business* and is committed to being brilliant at it. While most people investigating franchises examine the franchisor's effectiveness in distributing their products and services, few people determine whether or not the franchisor is skilled in the business of franchising.

How you identify a brilliant franchisor is to first identify how a franchisor makes money. Forgetting about any cash flow generated by company store operations, a typical franchisor makes money in only two or three different ways.

1. **Franchise fee revenue.** The franchisor charges franchisees upfront fees typically ranging from $20,000 to $40,000. This is not a big moneymaker to most franchisors. For the vast majority of franchisors this fee doesn't cover, or barely covers, the cost of running their internal franchise sales department. In other words, awarding you a franchise is typically a break-even proposition at best. By the time you write the franchisor a check for your franchise fee, chances are they have already spent that money in advertising and departmental costs trying to find you. The most successful franchisors make most of their cash flow from royalties. This means they can only make it if you make it. Be wary of franchisors who take big upfront fees (over $50,000) but don't produce the results to justify this investment.

2. **Royalties.** Franchisees pay franchisors a percentage of their gross revenue typically ranging from 5 to 10 percent. Fees could be higher, but higher fees should reflect more services. Express Personnel, for instance, charges higher fees, but they manage the entire backroom payroll operation for their franchisees. On the other hand, some franchisors don't charge royalties. They just depend on proprietary product sales to their franchisees. A company like Merle Norman Cosmetics® fall into this category. Royalties are the lifeblood of a franchisor's business. Brilliant franchisors are in the business of maximizing royalty collections. To maximize royalty collections, they must first be brilliant at developing peak-performing franchisees. This means they win when you win.

3. **Products.** A minor group of franchisors are also vendors, selling proprietary products and services to their franchisees at a profit. Companies like Ben and Jerry's® have exclusive vendor relationships with their franchisees. Franchisors who make money selling products are generally in the minority. Having a franchisor

who is also an exclusive vendor isn't necessarily a bad thing, although it can be very limiting. If the franchisor's prices are competitive, the products are unique, proprietary, and don't run the risk of being obsolete, and they have a strong national distribution network (meaning they can effectively get your products to your front door in a cost-effective manner), this can even be a competitive advantage.

Out of these revenue streams, *royalties and, for those franchisors who are also vendors, product sales* should be most important to the franchisor. Again, be wary of franchisors whose financial statements show they need the franchise fee revenue in order to survive. They will be tempted and probably will succumb to the financial pressure of awarding franchises to marginal candidates who have a higher probability of failure. Franchisors whose franchisees fail will probably not survive as franchisors. A franchisee failure is a black mark against the brand for customers, suppliers, and other franchisees.

> If you find a franchisor in the business of maximizing royalty revenue, you've found a franchisor who gets the business they're in.

Who Butters Their Bread?

If a franchisor is really in the business of maximizing royalty revenue (and possibly driving product sales to their franchisees), how will they accomplish this? Who are they counting on? Don't peak-performing franchisees sell the most products and services to their customers, and therefore pay the highest royalties and purchase the most products from the franchisor? Don't peak-performing franchisees do a better job at making money for themselves, creating job satisfaction for themselves and their employees, and taking care of their customer's needs? For these franchisors to be successful, doesn't it mean they're committed to taking you along for the ride?

If a franchisor is in the business of maximizing royalty revenue, *there's only one way to get there.* They have to be brilliant at finding and creating peak-performing franchisees.

When asked, "What does it take to be a brilliant franchisor?" The CEO of a nationally known auto repair franchise said it takes genius in four distinct areas:

1. Recruiting top-quality franchise candidates
2. Developing these candidates into peak-performing franchisees
3. Building a strong franchisee community
4. Building a strong, identifiable brand (marketing)

If they are weak in any one of these four areas, they will stop growing and start sinking. If they sink, you may go down with the ship.

In this chapter, we will briefly describe what brilliant recruiting, training, supporting, and relationship-building looks like. We will provide much greater detail further in this work. Since there are plenty of books, classes, articles, and other resources that talk about brilliant marketing, we won't address marketing here.

Recruiting Top-Quality Franchise Candidates

Once, a bunch of veteran franchisee recruiters were together at a conference, huddled around a table discussing franchisee recruitment strategies. A vice president of franchise sales from a large, national automobile body repair and painting franchisor shared his views on franchisee recruitment.

"It's not my job to qualify franchise candidates," he stated. "I will give anyone their God-given right to fail." This person thought it was his responsibility to take money from anyone with the financial capital and interest in opening a business, regardless of their background, skills, and aptitudes. He absolved himself of all personal responsibility of how well the franchisees he recruited performed; instead he let "God" sort it out. This is a violation of franchising's sacred trust.

You may be surprised to learn how many franchisors award franchises to franchise candidates whom they wouldn't hire to manage the same business. These franchisors may not be malicious or consciously doing anything wrong, but they are, at the least, incompetent as franchisors. They are dangerous to you, themselves, their customers, their franchisees, and franchising as a whole.

Picture yourself applying for an important position in a company. During the interview, instead of asking you questions about your background, work history, qualifications, and your reasons for looking for a change, the person in charge merely tried to sell you on how great their industry, company, and job opportunity are and why you should immediately jump at the opportunity to work for them. What would you think? What feelings would you be left with? Would you immediately sign on, buying into their wonderful stories about the opportunity that exists or would you pause to think, "If this is such a great company and magnificent opportunity, why are they selling the job so hard? They don't know me, so how do they know I'm right for the job?"

Would the job appear credible? Would the company appear credible? Yet this is how some franchisors recruit franchisees.

A thorough, integrity-based franchisee selection process is one of the best indicators of a franchisor's future success and growth. As you investigate franchisors, only continue in the investigation process with franchisors who demonstrate the following:

1. They are dedicated to helping you determine whether or not your personal objectives can be met using their business model. *If your objectives can't be met with a high degree of probability, they will walk away from the deal.*

2. They have a clear understanding of the individual traits, background, and capital necessary to produce success within their business model. In other words, they know who wins and who loses.

3. They evaluate you in order to determine whether or not you match the profile of a successful franchisee. They don't ask questions to simply ask questions, to "schmooze," or to try to win your trust. They ask questions to determine whether or not you fit their success profile. They are only interested in doing business with those who will win and they say "no" to everyone else.

4. They have a candidate-friendly process. *They discard high-pressure sales techniques.*

5. They understand your goals and objectives. They assist you by either providing, or helping you acquire the information you need to accurately evaluate the probability that their business will produce the results you're looking for. They demand that you do the same.

6. They have a clear, step-by-step recruitment process. Both you and the franchisor know where you are in the process and what additional steps need to be taken. If they don't have a step-by-

step recruitment process, they probably don't have a clear, well-thought-out, easy-to-follow business model either. Dismiss them as an option.

For instance, Ben and Jerry's® ice cream franchisor only recruits a select group of the many possible franchisees who apply for their franchise, rather than selling franchises to anyone who inquires. Their interview process is one of the most thorough screening processes in franchising. If you were to go through their investigation process, you would have the experience of being interviewed, qualified, and studied. You have to earn this franchise. Not only does Ben and Jerry's® believe it's their obligation to protect the integrity of the Ben and Jerry's® business model, they also believe their franchise sales department is the front-line protector of the corporate social mission, which is their company's reason for being. Having money and skill alone doesn't cut it in the Ben and Jerry's® organization. You must have the appropriate financial backing, requisite business skills, desire to become a socially responsible corporate citizen (according to the Ben and Jerry's® definition of what that means), and be able to create a fun and exciting environment for others.

They go so far as to ask their candidates, "If you were a Ben and Jerry's® ice cream flavor, which flavor would you be and why?" People have responded with such clever answers as "I don't know which flavor I am, but I am working hard to avoid becoming 'Chubby Hubby.'" They pay attention to those people.

Those who blow that question off as irrelevant are "red flagged" as possibly being boring. Being boring will disqualify you as a Ben and Jerry's® franchisee. Why? *Ben and Jerry's® isn't in the ice cream business.* They are in the "fun, excitement, simple pleasure, community, and social responsibility" business. They rely on peak-performing fun, exciting and socially responsible franchisees to pull this off.

Franchisors like Ben and Jerry's®, who recruit franchisee candidates who are a good fit and have a high probability of success typically grow larger and offer their franchisees more stability than those who don't. Franchisors who accept marginal candidates have a high probability of failing and disappearing—perhaps taking you and your money with them.

Being a brilliant franchisee recruiter is only part of what it takes to become a brilliant franchisor. Brilliant franchisors know how to efficiently and effectively impart the success formula of their business to people with diverse backgrounds. They know who to give away the brilliance of their model to, helping them become peak performers.

Developing Peak-Performing Franchisees

Picture two men gathered around a broken-down car. One is a race car mechanic. Having built drag racers from the ground up, he appears to know everything that there is to know about cars. Aside from filling up the gas tank and occasionally replacing windshield wiper blades, the second man is helpless around cars. The two are standing next to each other, while looking under the hood of the car, trying to diagnose what the problem is.

Every engine part that twirls, spins, revs, squeaks, grinds, smells, or hisses gives the race car mechanic information, which will help him find the cause of the problem. Why? He has the characteristics of a master mechanic. In contrast, the same sights, sounds, and smells tell the other man nothing. Why? He didn't know anything to begin with.

Although the two are both looking at the same engine, *they aren't really looking at the same engine! Only one has the characteristics of a master mechanic.*

It's the same with franchising. Brilliant franchisors don't look at their business, their customers, their industry, franchisees, or even franchising the same way as those who don't experience the same level of success. Like the race car mechanic, they also possess the characteristics of a master.

If you were to ask the race car mechanic to teach you how to become a master mechanic, you might see him pause. Perhaps he wouldn't know how to teach you or even where to begin. Why? True masters are "unconsciously competent," meaning they have long stopped having to think about what they're good at and how they got there. They just do things right out of habit, without much thought and energy. The same "unconscious competence" which makes a race car mechanic a masterful mechanic may make him a lousy trainer of other mechanics. It's been a long time since he had to think about what he was doing. He would probably have a hard time communicating what he does and how he does it to someone who doesn't already know.

Franchisors also fall into this trap.

The Training Trap

Any franchisor worth considering was at one time brilliant at operating the same business model they're now marketing as a franchise opportunity. Hopefully, they were so brilliant, like the race car mechanic, they no longer had to spend tremendous amounts of energy thinking about how to execute their business model. They just executed.

Every company that chooses franchising as their expansion model, finds themselves in a position of having to train people with no industry experience. The same "unconscious competence" that makes a franchisor a great executer of their business model may make them "unconsciously incompetent" in their ability to effectively transfer their knowledge and experience to people from outside their industry. In other words, the best executers run the risk of being the lousiest trainers. If a franchisor runs highly successful corporate-owned locations, be impressed but don't be enamored. Be enamored only when you've determined that they have a long track record of helping people just like you do the same.

Peak-performing franchisors understand this "brilliant executer-lousy trainer" paradox and have made great efforts to become competent trainers. They start by remembering what they're good at and then put their business's success formula down on paper in the form of an operations manual. Peak-performing franchisors have mastered how to quickly and efficiently transfer the success formula of their business model to qualified people from outside their industry in the form of initial and ongoing training and support.

Why Training is Overrated

Training is often defined as "knowledge transfer." But knowledge, left standing alone, doesn't make a difference. Why do so many teenagers pick up smoking? Don't they know smoking causes cancer? Why are so many American adults obese? Don't they know how to eat a salad and exercise? It seems that just knowing isn't working.

There's often a great divide between what people know and what they do. Peak-performing franchisees often don't know more than their average or underperforming counterparts. They simply implement more of the knowledge they all possess.

Knowing What to Do and Doing What You Know

Brilliant franchisors understand your great "knowing-doing" divide and are committed to stand in the gap on your behalf. Through their ongoing training and support programs, they will hold you accountable for consistently executing their knowledge to the best of your ability. By helping you to close your gap, they create two positive outcomes. First, you become a peak-performing franchisee who achieves a level of success you couldn't achieve on your own. Additionally, the franchisor maximizes their royalty collections, *which is the business they're in.*

We will discuss how to determine whether or not franchisors are excellent in training and support later in this book. However, the bottom line is: franchisees just like you are winning according to your definition of winning.

Building a Strong Franchisee Community

Brilliant franchisors don't stop at building peak-performing franchisees. While your peak individual performance is critical to both yours and the franchisor's success, franchising is a team sport. Brilliant franchisors know how to get fiercely independent franchisees with diverse backgrounds working together as a fully functioning unit. They make decisions based not only on what's in the franchisor's best interest, but what's in the team's best interest. They carefully weigh their decisions against the impact on the franchisee community.

As we've already said, like the McDonald's® Big Mac, most of a franchisor's million-dollar ideas will come from the franchisees. Brilliant franchisors know this. Their franchisee community becomes their idea farm. Franchisees of brilliant franchisors have the experience of being heard. They see their ideas implemented.

Great franchisors create opportunities to bring franchisees together to share and harvest their collective genius. They do this through such venues as conferences, business meetings, newsletters, conference calls, and intranet chat rooms.

Franchisees experience being connected to both their franchisor and the other franchisees. They have an experience of being part of an exclusive community dedicated to their success.

If you read the terms of most franchise agreements, you'll see that franchisors and franchisees are under no legal or business obligation to create or join such a community. This community transcends any existing legal or business relationship. Yet this community brings out the best in what franchisees and franchisors have to offer each other.

To be a franchisee of one home remodeling franchisor, you must first pass "The Camping Test." If the leadership team cannot picture themselves sitting around the campfire with you, roasting marshmallows and enjoying a deep personal conversation, you won't be awarded a franchise. Whether or not you enjoy the outdoors is irrelevant to The Camping Test. Whether or not the leadership team and the other franchisees will enjoy your company is. This franchisor has a community to protect.

Summary

As you're beginning to see, although franchisors are in the business of distributing products and services, franchising is a business unto itself. Aside from being brilliant at distributing their brand of products or services, a franchisor must be brilliant in the business of franchising. The business of franchising can be broken down into four key areas. The first is franchisee recruitment. Franchisors have to know how to recruit qualified franchise candidates. Second, franchisors must be brilliant in training and developing franchisees into peak performers. The good news is that a franchisor's survival depends on their ability to help you win. Third, they need to build a solid community, where the franchisor can harvest the collective genius of the franchisee community for the benefit of all. Lastly, they have either created a brand that means something to customers, or they have a proven plan for franchisees to follow, which will create such a brand. You should look into making investments with franchisors who get this. At its best, franchising transcends any legal or business relationship that exists between the franchisee and franchisor. A franchise is a community, comprised of franchisees, franchisors, and their employees, and suppliers, each looking out for the other's best interest and committed to the success of all.

What to Expect from the Next Chapter

You will take a more extensive look at the reasons why people invest in franchises. You will hear stories about people who moved forward with different franchises and explore what they expected to happen versus what actually happened when they got started. We will also compare the profiles and explore the differences between the people who take control over their own futures by investing in a franchise versus those who return to the workforce.

Chapter 2

Why Should I Invest in a Franchise?

People often ask us, "Why should I invest in a franchise?" We will give you the short answer now, and more details throughout this chapter. A 1997 Gallup study showed that 94 percent of franchisees consider themselves successful. Consider that this response is based on the franchisees' definition of success, which would include achieving more of such things as:

- Money
- Time
- Work-life balance
- Flexibility
- Challenge
- Control
- Security and stability
- Equity
- Making a difference in the lives of others
- Personal responsibility
- Personal impact on the bottom line

In the same study, 75 percent of franchisees polled said knowing what they know now, they would make the same decision again. In contrast, if you asked your co-workers and peers the same questions, how many of them would say they are successful? How many of them would choose the same career or company again? The simple answer is people invest in franchises because most franchisees win.

Now we have a question for you. If most franchisees win and most of them would make the same decision again why do as many as 99 percent of people who investigate franchising decide not to invest?

The Path of the 99 Percent

Purely statistically speaking (and nothing personal intended), it's almost certain you won't make an investment in a franchise either. You will probably complain about the way things are, dream about what could be, take a brief stand for yourself by declaring, "I'm tired of making money for others. Now it's my turn!" Maybe you'll "Google" different franchise opportunities, visit franchisor home pages, gather stacks of franchisor brochures, research companies, talk to trusted people and professionals, and have conversations with various franchise opportunities. You will feel proactive. You will tell your friends you're considering buying a business. Chances are they thought about it too. Some will be happy for you, some will be jealous, some will be afraid for you. Virtually everyone will share their strong opinions. You'll dream about what it would be like to be your own boss. You will think about your customers and employees. You will make clever little charts such as the "T-Bar," where you neatly list all the "pros" on the left side of the page, balanced by the "cons" on the right side. Then the time will come to make a decision. Fear, doubt, and negative self-chatter (yours, your spouse's, your kids,' your parents,' your friends', and your hired professionals') will kick into high gear. Eventually, you will probably make a fear-based "no" decision, backed by the logic of your neatly listed "cons."

"The business has fatal flaws," you think. "Employee turnover is too high. Competition is too fierce. The business is too risky. Sure, it may work in some areas, but everyone knows our town is different." And with everything going on in your life, the timing couldn't be worse. Yes, you are being completely responsible with your resources. You didn't work this hard and long and sacrifice this much to lose what you have earned. Moving forward with a franchise would put your family in danger. If you leave your company, you will lose your insurance benefits and 401(k). What if someone in your family had to go to a hospital? How would you survive without insurance? Plus, your industry is changing so fast, in a few years your expertise would be obsolete and it would be impossible for you to regain entry if your business didn't make it. Certainly almost every reasonable person armed with the same research and faced with the same personal challenges you have would naturally come to the same conclusion.

And you are right.

Ninety-nine percent do.

The Path of the 1 Percent

The 1 percent and the 99 percent all start in the same physical place in the franchise investigation process. However, they don't all start in the same clean mental place. Truth be known, and this is going to make some people crazy, the 99 percent have a consistent and persistent career complaint with no real intention of ever doing anything about it. This isn't right or wrong, just the way it is. The 1 percent have the same complaints as do the 99 percent, just different future intentions. The 99 percent investigates franchises with the underlying intention of disproving different franchise opportunities so they can dismiss self-employment as a career option, and go back to a career that seems to keep choosing them rather than a career they choose. Conversely, the 1 percent makes a firm commitment to put the past in the past and alter the future.

If you are among the 1 percent, with or without *Street Smart Franchising*, you will probably find a way to make your life and career work in franchising, evidenced by the fact that 94 percent of franchisees consider themselves successful.

Starting a franchise is an unreasonable and unnatural undertaking. But the 1 percent refuses to live a reasonable, natural, and compromised life. Their circumstances aren't any different than yours. Many have similar backgrounds, finances, experience, education, and training. They are your age, have the same family challenges, and even live in your neighborhood. They don't have more confidence, skills, education, experience, or capital than you. Perhaps they are more committed to their dreams. Perhaps they simply have more pain.

Whatever their reason, they have come to a place in their life where they would rather take a shot and fail than sit in the bleachers and wonder what it's like to play.

Late at night, the 1 percent has fast-forwarded to the end of their life or career and envisions themselves sitting in a rocking chair in front of their fireplace thinking, "My career didn't make a difference." They have been to retirement parties and seen plaques and gold watches handed out to the retiring department heads and co-workers. They have heard the toastmasters deliver different versions of the same sincere speeches, like "We will always miss you," and "The office will never be the same without you." They also saw how these retirees were always replaced and seldom missed. They don't want to end their career in the banquet room at a steakhouse, with a smiling waiter bringing out a sheet cake with strawberry fruit filling with the words "Happy Retirement!!!!" neatly printed in all capital letters and punctuated with several exclamation points for extra sincerity. They cringe at the thought of slightly buzzed co-workers breaking out into an out-of-tune chorus of "(S)He's a jolly good fellow." Then it's all over. Their career ends as uneventfully as it started. They think, "All the sacrifice. All the hard work. All the time away from my family. For what?"

This potential future spooks the 1 percent into positive action in the present. They refuse to be the person who ends their career this way. They are going to work and live all out, holding back nothing in reserve.

The Voice of the Inner Critic

The 99 percent aren't worse than the 1 percent, nor are they designed some way they aren't supposed to be. As the song aptly states, they are "good fellows which nobody can deny."

However, the 99 percent are more likely than the 1 percent to listen to the lies of their "Inner Critic." You know him. He stays in the background, whispering what you desperately wish not to be true,

25

but on some level believe anyway. Your Inner Critic waits in ambush, ready to emotionally hijack you at your weakest moments and seize control of your decision-making capabilities. Now you are contemplating a life-changing transition. The Critic loves such change. Change and ambiguity are the bread and water he needs to survive. Life changes offer the Critic an opportunity to create a larger speaking platform. He's been quiet for so long, now it's his turn to shout and he has you convinced it's your turn to listen. Then he hurls new versions of the same old accusations he's always made against you.

- You aren't good enough.
- You aren't smart enough.
- You fail at everything.
- You are helpless.
- You are poor.
- You are worthless.
- Nobody cares about you.
- You can't trust anyone.
- You will never get what you want.
- You don't deserve it.
- You don't belong.
- You don't make a difference.
- There is something wrong with you.
- It's all your fault.
- You'll go broke.
- You are weak.
- You can't do it.

"And that's the way it is always going to be until the day you die. So forget it," says the Critic.

Since the situation is new, once again, you fear the Critic is right and you listen. And in the end, instead of buying a franchise and pursuing a life you desire, you buy the Critic's lie and relive some version of the same old past you expressed a sincere desire to leave behind. You will compromise on your future and a small part of you will die.

Yes, 99 percent of you who are reading this book will probably make a fear-based, Critic-inspired decision and back it up with conventional logic. You think such things as, "I need the security of a

job until my kids go to college. This business has too much competition." Or, "The business isn't proven (because it doesn't have
enough competition). Employees goof off. Employees rob you blind.
Employees will leave you for another 50 cents an hour. I know someone who failed in a similar business. There's too much inventory.
My spouse isn't supporting me." And then you take a pass.

However, you still hold on to the thought, "If I could only find
the right business, I could become successful."

The "Right" Business

You know the right business. The one with little or no start-up costs.
You could start it with the loose change you found in your sofa cushions. There is no inventory. Or if there is inventory, customers will
pay you first, and then you can go out and buy your inventory with
your customers' money. There are no contingent liabilities such as
real estate or equipment leases. There's little risk, a big return on
investment, and fast equity build-up. You parlay your sofa cushion
money into a million-dollar enterprise.

Although there's no competition, there's lots of demand for your
products and services all year long. People will walk through snow
drifts in bare feet just for the opportunity to buy from you. And your
business is safe. No one has ever failed in this franchise before. Your
products and services are so unique they can't be found anywhere
else. Plus the franchisor holds the patent, so no one ever will. Banks
think the business is so hot they are lined up to offer you money on
a signature with no collateral. However, you don't need banks. Just
more old sofa cushions to rummage through.

And think about your customers! They are happy, repeat customers, the kind of customers who walk into your place of business
with hundred-dollar bills hanging out of their pockets and buy every
product you offer. Plus, they bring other customers with them. Of
course they seek you out based on your reputation alone, so there's
never a need to advertise, network, sell, or even leave the comfort of
your home to find them.

What about your employees? There are no employees needed! Or
if you do need employees, there won't be any turnover. They punch
in exactly when they are supposed to, and do what you tell them

exactly the way you told them to do it. Therefore, they need little supervision. They open, close, and maintain your operation while creating complete customer satisfaction. You only need to show up to empty the cash register. Unfortunately, the register fills up so often, this may require you to make several trips a day to the bank, which can interfere with your golf game.

If by some freak chance you do have to replace an employee, it will be a breeze because responsible, clean-cut potential employees with positive "can do" attitudes are always knocking on your door, looking to come to work for you.

What's more, this business is easy to run—the learning curve is nearly nonexistent. You come out of the initial training a master. You make no costly mistakes. You work 9 to 5 with no weekends. You finish one year making the same or more than you're earning now. And next year you'll double your income.

Plus, all this happens just at the right time in your life to start a business. You know the right time. The 99 percent live an illusion that the universe is comprised of two time periods to start a business: the "right time" and the time period they're currently living in, which of course is the wrong time.

The "Right Time" to Start a Business

1. Your kids have to be the right age. They aren't too old. They aren't too young. Or they got old and moved out. Or if only you didn't have kids. Certainly nobody has ever found a way to have kids your age and succeed in franchising at the same time.
2. You are the right age. Either you are older, financially secure, and have money to risk. Or you are middle-aged, a good earner, and at a pivot point in your life. Or you are younger, have little money, and nothing to lose. Certainly nobody your age has ever succeeded in franchising.
3. Your parents are the right age. They are young enough where they don't need your support. Or your parents are old and secure enough to support you by giving you some money. Or you no longer have parents. Certainly nobody with parents at

their stage in life has ever succeeded in franchising.

4. You have to have the right spouse. He or she earns enough to meet your household expenses and wholeheartedly supports whatever decision you make. Or your spouse will help you in business to keep your overhead down. Or you aren't married and don't have those commitments. Certainly no one in your current marital situation has ever succeeded in franchising.

5. You can make time. Either you have free time at work with which to explore your options or you got laid off and are having trouble finding a job. Certainly no one with your time commitments has ever succeeded in franchising.

So what do the Boogey Man, The Lost Continent of Atlantis, The Right Franchise, and The Right Time to Start a Business all have in common?

There are no such things.

Looking for the perfect business to start at the right time is the franchising equivalent of going on a "snipe hunt." Remember snipe hunts? For those of you who don't know, on camping vacations and family picnics, sometimes the adults send kids out to find a snipe, in order to get rid of them for a while so they can drink beer, play cards, and swear.

The 99 percent hold on to the fallacy that there's a perfect business which can be started at the right time. The 1 percent know they have to go out and create the right business and make it the right time.

The Differences Between the 1 Percent and 99 Percent

The 99%	The 1%
Waits for the "right time" to start a business.	Declares "Now is the time." And then works to make it the right time.
Tries to find the perfect business.	Tries to find a solid business and will work to make it the right business for them.

The 99%	The 1%
Looks for what's wrong with franchises and reasons they won't work.	Looks for franchises with a strong track record of success, while acknowledging their unique challenges and potential pitfalls.
Is normal and reasonable.	Is exceptional and unreasonable.
Is committed to achieving stability and security and is risk-averse.	Is committed to making a difference with their life and career and is willing to accept risk to do so.
Is afraid of the unknown. Make their fears mean "something is wrong" and back away from creating the future they desire.	Is afraid of the unknown. Doesn't make their fears mean anything. "I am afraid of the unknown," they think, "so what else is new?"
Their future is something which happens to them and they fall into.	Their future is something they design and then live into.
Listens to the opinions and accusations of the Inner Critic. Lets him impact their decision-making.	Listens to the opinions and accusations of The Inner Critic. Doesn't let him impact their decision making.
Isn't born into the 99 percent. Becomes the 99 percent through the decisions they make.	Isn't born into the 1 percent. Becomes the 1 percent through the decisions they make.

How to Join the 1 Percent

- Recognize that if you haven't already started a business or franchise, or lived off 100 percent performance-based compensation, you are already in the 99 percent.
- Recognize the 1 percent isn't better or worse than the 99 percent, just different. There's nothing wrong with being in the 99 percent.
- Recognize your past is a product of the decisions you made earlier. You may not be happy with your decisions or the results, but you accept the past as a product of your own creation.
- You look into the future. What will your life be like if you stay on your predictable course? What will your life and career look like five years from now? Ten? Twenty? What will your

life and career have stood for? What will you have accomplished? What would still be left to accomplish? Hang out with this future. Picture it so clearly it's as if you're already living it. Visit this future often. Know what it will be like before you get there.

- Think about what you "must have" in life, where not having these things is not an option. For example, "My kids must go to college." "I must own a home in a safe neighborhood." Identify the goals which, if not achieved, would make you feel your life was a monumental failure. Are you on track to achieve your "must haves"? If not, you are on the road to serious regret.

- Think about your "want to haves," those things which, although desired, are not mission-critical and you could find a way to live without them and are actually living without them now. Examples would include a bigger house, a nicer car, better vacations, etc. Think about which "want to haves" you will predictably have and which you won't.

Creating a Desired Future

Use Table 2-1 on the next page as a worksheet to start designing your future.

- Prioritize according to the following 5-point scale.
- Make a decision as to whether or not your predictable future is acceptable or unacceptable.
- If the future is acceptable, more power to you. You are winning! You're living a fabulous life, designing a life you want. What more can you ask for? You may not have everything you want, but clearly you are realizing your high priorities and maintaining the integrity of your values. A new business may or may not improve the quality of your life. Investigate franchises carefully. Evaluate how a franchise will impact your future. Make sure your "must haves" in life are intact and a franchise will deliver more of your "want to haves" than your current course.
- Investigate franchising as a strategy to possibly win bigger.

$$\longleftrightarrow$$

| 1 | 2 | 3 | 4 | 5 |

I could live without. I wish for, but could live without. I can't live without.

My future desires	Rate from 1–5	Assuming nothing changes, what is the likelihood I will achieve this desire in the future? (impossible, not likely, very likely, almost certain)	Am I OK with this likelihood? (Yes/ No)

Table 2-1. Figuring out your future

If your future is unacceptable, you are faced with two decisions:

1. **Accept the unacceptable.** Let go of your future desires and accept what is. Accept the results of this decision because it's your decision, nobody is doing it to you. It's through your acceptance that the unbearable will become bearable. If you accept the results of your decision *as the results of your decision*, you won't feel like a loser.

2. **No longer accept the unacceptable.** This is a life-changing decision; one of the most powerful decisions you can make. This is a decision to put the past in the past, and by doing so it will immediately alter and enlarge your future. This decision will energize you, calling you forward into committed action, altering what is possible for you.

If you decide to no longer accept the unacceptable, you are on the path to greater success, meaning, and achievement. Before you begin down this path, we will equip you with the following:

- Greater self-awareness of your style and gifts and your predictable value to a franchise opportunity (Chapter 4)
- Clearly stated and well-prioritized personal goals (Chapter 5)
- A greater understanding of exactly what it takes to win in franchising (Chapter 6)
- Knowledge and understanding of the learning curve franchisees go through as they take on a new venture. Strategies to accelerate your learning curve (Chapter 7)

Only after you have read these chapters and developed a clear understanding of franchising in general will we take you through a process of identifying and investigating your options (Chapters 8 and 9). Remember our agreement and read Chapter 3 next and resist the temptation to jump around. Franchising is about producing great results by following proven processes and systems. Although you may not know where we're going with every chapter, we have a 30-year track record of getting people there! Have faith! Take one step at a time. Congratulations on taking this powerful step.

Chapter 3

Understanding Your Behavior Style

Chapter Objectives

- To help you accurately assess which one or two of the four possible behavior styles you use to produce results.
- To help you predict your areas of genius as well as weaknesses and potential threats before you invest in a franchise opportunity.
- To coach you in how to determine whether or not your style matches a franchisor's profile of a successful franchisee.

Behavior Styles

In the early 1920s an American psychologist named William Moulton Marston sought to create a model that would allow him to predict and explain how emotionally healthy people react to both situations and other people. To test the accuracy of his new theories of behavior, Marston needed to create a system of measurement. Incorporating some of famed psychologist Carl Jung's personality theories describing four distinct personality and behavior styles, Marston created an assessment tool that measured the following behavioral characteristics:

1. **D**ominance
2. **I**nfluence
3. **S**teadiness
4. **C**ompliance

Dominance measures how people respond to challenges and problems. People who are high on dominance will attack problems head on and seek out potential problems before they occur. People who are low on dominance will display a tendency to let events unfold and see what happens before responding.

Influence measures how people respond to interactions with others. People who are high on influence are very outgoing and have a need to build strong personal relationships and influence others with their views. People who are low on influence will appear as more distant and private.

Steadiness measures how people respond to the pace of their environment. People who are high on steadiness desire predictable and slower-paced environments where they can see projects from the beginning through to completion. People low on steadiness desire change and like to multi-task.

Compliance measures how people respond to structure or rules created by others. People who are high on compliance thrive in highly structured environments where they know exactly what to do and what's expected of them. People low on compliance like to make their own rules and prefer to be self-managed. Take a wild guess where entrepreneurs are on this scale. Most entrepreneurs are a "don't tell me what to do," waiting to happen.

It's from these four characteristics that the DISC theory and assessment tool was named. Marston proved that those who possess similar characteristics also happen to speak, listen, process information, make decisions, and produce results in similar fashion.

DISC has become one of the most widely used, statistically validated, and universally accepted behavior assessments that companies use to determine whether or not the skills people possess match what is required for particular positions, including franchise ownership. We believe that the DISC theory is among the best available tools to help you evaluate whether or not your skills match a franchisor's profile of a successful franchisee. We will explain the DISC theory in a moment.

As you contact different franchise companies and get further into their franchise sales process, you'll find that some highly skilled and sophisticated franchisors have already used DISC or a similar instrument to statistically measure and help create their composite profile of a successful franchisee. They have figured out who wins and who doesn't. They will profile you on the same instrument, compare your results against their composite of a successful franchisee, and examine the deviations. They will discuss the deviations with you and how these deviations may play out positively or negatively in your own business. For instance, they may see that you are more introverted than their profile of a successful franchisee and they may ask you whether or not you're willing to cold call for customers. Some franchisors put so much emphasis on these instruments they will use them to qualify or disqualify applicants for a franchise. Other franchisors take a more balanced approach, using their findings with other information they gather, such as interviews, applications, past results, resumes, and financial statements.

Many smaller chains have too few franchisees to make a statistical sampling relevant. Larger, more unsophisticated franchise chains may assume they already know and may not see the value in using instruments. Expect them to supply you with anecdotal evidence, which we urge you to listen to, but to not completely trust. Not that these franchisors are knowingly misleading you or doing anything wrong. It's that they are making educated guesses using observational data that may or may not be accurate. People have a tendency to see what they want to see and to ignore the rest. Create your own profile using the information in this chapter. The genius of the DISC theory is that it's both easy to learn and apply. You will be a DISC expert in about 15 minutes.

DISC theory states the obvious; normal and emotionally healthy people display consistent and predictable patterns of behavior. Taken one step further, people with similar styles within the same franchise system have a tendency to produce similar results. The top performers generally display one style and underperformers display another.

Seldom will you find style similarities between top performers and underperformers.

Before we get into styles, understand that we're not saying that one particular style of performance is better than another style as it relates to franchising in general. We are, however, asserting that franchise systems are typically set up to support certain styles of performance and not others, which is one reason why franchisees' performance varies within the same franchise system.

Think about it. Franchise systems are typically created by the successful entrepreneurs who invented these systems. Put another way, every *franchise system* at one time was an entrepreneur's *personal system*, usually started with a single business unit. Unless the franchisor's systems have undergone years of development, evolution, or transformation, the franchise system will still reflect the entrepreneur's original personal system. Since each entrepreneur is dominant in one style or another, doesn't it stand to reason that franchisees whose behavior styles most resemble the original entrepreneur's style will also be the ones most likely to master this system? Additionally, many franchisors simply don't take into account style differences when they create systems and develop training programs. They create, train, and develop according to their own dominant style the same way other people act according to their own dominant style.

Certainly, there are other mitigating factors that impact a franchisee's performance and which you will also need to take into account, such as demographics, market penetration, brand awareness, competition, location, capitalization, and general economic conditions. However, don't discount style. Behavior styles do play a role in determining results. If your style more closely matches the profile of an underperformer rather than that of a performer, all other things being equal, you run a high risk of being an underperformer yourself regardless of your past successes. Why? Because the role the franchise plays in a particular business may not offer you your ideal work environment or the "highest and best" use of your talents.

Have you ever had a job which didn't fit you, where your weaknesses were exposed, and your gifts weren't utilized? Chances are you produced mediocre results at best and went home exhausted. Work was hard and frustrating. You felt like you were always pushing a rock uphill. Each morning, when your alarm clock sounded, you probably threw a shoe at it and fought the urge to bury your head in your pillow and go back to sleep. And when you finally did get out of bed, pity the poor souls who were unlucky or stupid enough to cross your path or get in your way.

Conversely, have you ever worked in a job which seemed tailor-made for you? Work became play. Chances are you produced great results with seemingly little effort. You lived and worked in a perpetual state of forward momentum. After the work day was over, you actually went home energized. When your alarm went off the next morning, you jumped out of bed, ready to take on the day. Sometimes you even beat the alarm clock up, in anticipation of another great day. You were floating in such joyous exuberance that other, more miserable people fantasized about clipping your wings and punching you in the mouth.

Isn't this last experience what you're looking to re-create with a franchise? Don't you want work that's so interesting and challenging you welcome every day that you're called forth into action? Don't you want work to be play? Don't you want to inspire your friends, family, and associates to find their own nirvana?

Use the information in this chapter to help you determine whether or not a particular franchise opportunity will provide you with your ideal work environment, setting you up to win.

Again, don't expect every franchisor to know who wins and who loses and why. Most have a high belief level in their program and are sold on their own opportunity. Additionally, many will chalk up franchisees' wins to the brilliance of the franchise system and franchisees' losses to the shortcomings of the franchisees. In the same way, many franchisees will chalk up their personal victories to their own expertise and their failures to failures in the franchise system. Reality is usually buried somewhere in the middle. By learning and applying the simple techniques you will learn in this chapter, you will gain keen insights into what it takes to succeed in any given franchise system.

While you can't rely on your personal style to identify which particular industries you should be looking at inside of franchising, your style will help you determine which specific companies, cultures, and work environments you should and should not consider. And while you can't use the information in this chapter to determine whether or not you belong in a particular industry, it will help you both match your profile against the profile of a successful franchisee of a specific business and whether or not you are a fit for a given franchisor's corporate culture. Put another way, while you can't use this information to determine whether or not you should be in a foodservice or hair care business, it will help you determine whether you are a fit for such specific chains as Subway® or Great Clips.®

How Does DISC Work?

The DISC instrument validates that people are very consistent in how they speak, listen, and react to people and situations. So consistent in fact, people have essentially become typecast actors in their own movies, playing the same character again and again. Although people and events are not predictable, the way people react to other people and events is predictable and can even be measured with a shocking degree of accuracy. To assist you, we have applied movie characterizations to each of the four styles.

In this chapter, you will identify which one or two of the four possible typecast characters both you and others play. This will help you to predetermine which characters excel and which underachieve in any given franchise system. The four typecast actors are as follows:

- The Action Hero
- The Comedian
- The Faithful Sidekick
- The Private Eye

You Are an Action Hero If ...

You're an outgoing, hard-charging, risk-taking, task-oriented, efficient, disciplined, organized, results-oriented, and "take charge" character. You make quick, emotional, instinctual, or gut-based decisions rather than information-based or logic-based decisions. Attaining goals, assuming control, achieving results, accepting personal challenges, and creating efficiency drives Action Heroes. You speak pointedly and directly, telling it like it is. You possess strong opinions and are often closed to any new facts and information that may contradict previously formed opinions. Because Action Heroes don't need or seek much information to make their quick decisions, you have difficulty listening to details, preferring instead to listen to headlines, highlights, or the bottom line. As a result, Action Heroes are often perceived as poor listeners. Since you are such a strong personality, you can easily bowl over weaker personality types, creating conflict in the process. You may fear being taken advantage of, so you may often question the personal motives, integrity, and loyalty of others, creating issues around trust.

Your Value in Business

You are results-oriented and focused on the goal. You seldom lose sight of your goals or the big picture. You know what you're looking to accomplish and generally are keyed in as to how to get there. You seldom deviate from your stated objectives. You also get others around you focused and organized.

You are strategic and tactical. You know to chunk problems and situations down to their simplest forms and quickly create a plan of attack. You know how to simplify everything with little effort.

You are visionary. You can see past the minutia of the day-to-day operations of a business and hold on to your original vision. You are excellent at stating your vision to others in simple terms so they also get it. You always seem to have one eye on what's occurring and another eye on the bottom line. Others will follow you because of both your commanding presence and clear and simple ideas of what's required to win.

You are an efficiency expert. You know how to trim the fat and cut the waste. You are always identifying and pushing for the quickest, easiest, simplest, and most efficient way to produce results. You will quickly identify and spend time executing the activities that drive results. You know which buttons need to be pushed and when, and can be counted on to push those buttons.

You are responsible, self-directed, and self-managed. You do what you say you're going to do. As long as you know what the results need to look like at the end of the day, you have an uncanny ability to make things happen. Against all odds, you seem to invent ways to produce results and win.

You are a natural-born leader. You have a forceful personality and appear to others as an authority figure. People naturally follow your lead.

You get involved. You see it as your duty to look beyond what's occurring in your little franchise and contribute on a regional or national level. You want to be heard and your opinions are generally worth listening to.

You have a strong operational focus. You know how to implement processes and systems to produce results.

You possess an excellent ability to multi-task. You know how to juggle people and tasks without dropping any balls. You have a natural ability to keep multiple ideas in front of you without having to write things down.

You create win-win solutions. You are very skilled at identifying what winning looks like for yourself and others and will work to create solutions where everyone gets what they want.

You have great problem-solving ability. You don't shrink from, avoid, or deny conflicts and challenges. You attack head on without reservation. You will be the first to identify where potential breakdowns are occurring or may occur in the future and are often ready with a solution.

You are action-oriented and quick to implement. Once you decide what to do, you don't let any grass grow under your feet. You are in perpetual motion. You get more done than most people and in less time.

You aren't afraid to take risks. As such, yours is the most entrepreneurial behavior style. You aren't afraid to spend time or money when necessary to create long-term gains.

You are a strong decision maker. You move quickly and decisively and aren't prone to second-guess yourself or waffle when making important decisions. Once you decide, it's full steam ahead.

You have a commonsense approach to business. You can easily frame any given situation and quickly formulate a plan of attack. You are brilliant at looking past symptoms and getting to the heart or source of the matter.

You put forth a heroic effort and play to win. You expect and demand the same of others. No one working with you is allowed a free pass.

What Will Kill You If You Aren't Careful

You have a tendency to resist external controls. You may not value being held accountable to following a system. You resist following certain operational procedures if you deem them inefficient or cumbersome. You will be tempted to deviate from a franchise system, increasing your risk and decreasing the franchisor's ability to offer you meaningful support. You don't always respect boundaries.

You form strong opinions and resist checking out perceptions against the facts. You may make poor decisions because of lack of information. You aren't always open to receive information that's contrary to what you believe. Because you like to rally others to your point of view, the franchisor and other franchisees can label you as a "rebel" or "troublemaker" and you can lose credibility with the franchisor. Because you stop listening once your mind is made up, it can be difficult for a franchisor to train and support you and point out problem areas in your business.

You seek to control situations or interactions. You struggle to follow other leaders. You may butt heads with franchisor leadership and alienate yourself from the franchisor and other franchisees.

You attempt to gain the upper hand in negotiations. You may be perceived as selfish and not a team player which will get in the way of others wanting to help you.

You tell others what's on your mind without a thought as to how others might react to it. You can damage key franchisee-franchisor relationships if others aren't comfortable with your directness or bluntness.

You have a tendency to challenge, confront, and make others look wrong, which again can diminish your franchisor's ability to provide you with leadership.

You possess a tendency to change systems, processes, and procedures that you didn't create or with which you don't agree. You run the risk of changing the franchise system before you ever learn it, which could create costly mistakes and extend your learning curve.

You are a notoriously poor listener. This can get in the way of your training and development and create personality conflicts with a franchise's support staff.

You are a strong leader and have a tendency to bowl over weaker personalities. Many franchise support and training professionals possess those weaker personalities, and your behavior can damage key relationships.

At times you will risk damaging key relationships to get what you want since you are more about achieving great results than building powerful relationships.

You have a tendency to dominate and micromanage others, which may create employee turnover, halting forward momentum.

You have a tendency to delegate without effectively training others, setting employees up to fail.

You have a temper. Employees with weaker personality types may hide mistakes and information that indicate problems just to avoid setting you off. You are so intolerant of mistakes, you may not give your employees the safe space necessary to make them learn their roles.

You like to be in control and make decisions with little feedback. You may not effectively harness the collective genius of your employees.

You take a "ready-fire-aim" approach to business. You may impulsively act without thinking about all the ramifications of your actions.

You are a natural risk-taker, which will help you. You may take foolish chances, which can hurt you.

You are impatient and want things now. You will sometimes force a result rather than let it happen naturally. You err on the side of aggressiveness.

You forget to give others positive affirmation for a job well done. You have a tendency to communicate to your employees only when you spot a problem, giving some the experience of being unappreciated, which will create turnover.

Your Ideal Franchise ...

Has freedom to make unit-level strategic decisions. The franchise system isn't completely button-downed and handed down from the top.

Contains business systems that are clearly articulated, efficient, and well thought-out.

Offers you a work environment that's efficient and well organized.

Involves multi-tasking and change. Every day is a bit different.

Includes work days that allow for flexibility.

Requires great personal challenge and working on the big picture. You may appreciate a smaller franchisor who doesn't have it all figured out yet. Or a smaller, more entrepreneurial franchise where you have direct access to the decision makers.

Is a proven, replicable business model, not just a good idea.

Contains strong management information systems and clear key measures of success.

Isn't loosey-goosey, where key management doesn't have the skill or experience to continue on a growth track.

Offers customers a unique product or service that demonstrates value, one that will produce great results for customers or clients, and is something you can sell with integrity.

Is cutting- or leading-edge.

Is a system that provides easy access to data and key indicators of the business.

Offers access to the franchisor's decision makers and a forum to voice opinions.

If successful, can continually be grown.

Is run by executives with a participatory leadership style.

Leaves you alone and won't be overly involved in your business.

Fits the profile of a higher-risk franchise offering you the possibility for growth and higher return.

Gives you choices and flexible "wiggle room," not mandates.

You Are a Comedian If ...

You are fun-loving, outgoing, empathetic, risk-taking, people-oriented, charming, affable, creative, enthusiastic, talkative, optimistic, trusting, and highly influential. Like Action Heroes, Comedians are also instinctual, emotion- or gut-based rather than information-based decision makers. However, where Action Heroes are more task-oriented, Comedians are more people-oriented. Building quality relationships, having fun, and attaining social recognition drive them. Comedians look for reasons to believe in, trust, and like others. Like Action Heroes, they listen more attentively to headlines, highlights, the bottom line, and the big picture rather than the details. They have trouble saying "no," and have a tendency to over-promise. They struggle with details, are known to become disorganized, and have trouble managing their time effectively.

Your Value in Business

You have creative problem-solving ability. You are an out-of-the-box thinker. You can find new ways to look at problems and find solutions. You are resourceful and can find what has worked in other businesses and industries and synthesize a solution for your business.

You are visionary; you see the big picture. You can look beyond the status quo and see what is possible. You are skilled in enrolling others in your vision of the future.

You build consensus and will work hard to avoid conflict. You will work to build powerful relationships with the franchisor and other franchisees.

You are goal-oriented. You will work hard to attain your goals.

You influence others. You know how to rally the troops and inspire others to action.

You work well with others and function well on a team. You will work to build synergies and bond with the franchisor's employees.

You are a great communicator. You are easy to talk to and relate to. You know how to make customers and employees feel right at home. You build powerful life-long relationships with customers and employees.

You are optimistic and put forth positive energy. You maintain a healthy can-do attitude in the face of adversity.

You are trusting and can create trust in customers and employees.

You are outgoing and exhibit mastery in sales and marketing. You are a natural-born salesperson and promoter. You aren't afraid of getting out into the community and telling others why they should be doing business with you. You know how to drive sales.

You make work and shopping fun for employees and customers. Your energy is contagious.

You possess good customer service skills. You know how to keep customers satisfied and keep them coming back.

You are a democratic manager, good at soliciting feedback. You will work to create a positive experience for clients and customers alike.

You are entrepreneurial and a risk-taker. You aren't afraid to spend money to achieve your objectives.

You are quick to make decisions or to implement them.

You like change and you move fast. You can get much done in a short period of time.

You have a high degree of confidence in your own abilities.

What Will Kill You If You Aren't Careful

You move quickly. You don't always think about the total impact of your actions before you take them. You are a "run out in traffic before you look both ways" decision maker, which can cost you precious money and time. You need to learn how to solicit feedback from the franchise support staff so you don't get flattened in traffic.

You may resist following processes, which can dramatically increase your risk in business. You would rather be unrestricted in your movements to create a result. This will make it difficult for the franchisor to be able to support you properly as you would rather create your own system.

You seldom do the same thing twice. You are so creative; you're constantly inventing new ways to serve your customers. You run the risk of changing the winning formula, making yourself less effective. You need to learn how to create a business rhythm.

You form strong opinions and resist checking out perceptions against the facts. You just assume you're right and then take off.

You are very trusting and people may take advantage of you.

You are optimistic and may overlook information, which could indicate a problem. You miss opportunities to head off problems before they occur. You can confuse "feeling good" with creating great results.

You don't always say everything that's on your mind in order to avoid a conflict. You have a tendency to hold back "negative" information from people who can help you.

You make "gut-based" or "feelings-based" decisions and may dismiss facts if facts contrast with "feelings." You don't always check opinions against facts.

You will go off on tangents and waste time. You are so creative that you can lose your focus.

You are probably highly disorganized and typically weak with details and financial numbers. Your motto is "Data schmata! Let's go sell!"

You know how to spend money and may struggle with containing costs.

You may have a tendency to focus on the top line (revenues) and ignore the bottom line (cash flow).

Your Ideal Franchise ...

Is known for building rock-solid franchisee-franchisor relationships. Join a franchise which gives you ample opportunity to network with and learn from other franchisees.

Offers a product or service that you are passionate about, which you can enthusiastically market and sell.

Leverages your creativity and ability to build repeat customers.

Is your idea of a fun time.

Is informal in nature, highly entrepreneurial, and may resemble the culture of a family business.

Is led by a CEO with a democratic leadership style where you have the opportunity to voice your opinions.

Isn't a low margin/high transaction "penny profit" business, such as fast food, which relies on an owner's ability to tightly manage the cost side of the business. Your strengths are driving sales, not containing costs.

Is simplistic, structured, and methodical, compensating for your weak organizational skills.

Where advertising, sales, and promotion create a competitive point of difference, showcasing your natural abilities to sell, promote, and network within the community (such as the "quick sign" industry).

Is a "flashy" franchise with great "country club" appeal, which appeals to your ego.

Offers freedom from tight external controls; a franchise which lets their franchisees find their own way while at the same time maintains the integrity of the brand.

You Are a Faithful Sidekick If ...

You are a warm, dependable, good-natured, structured, methodical, systems-oriented, open-minded, consistent, persistent, level-headed, pragmatic, objective, sincere, and empathetic team player. Like Comedians, Faithful Sidekicks are people-oriented, but unlike Comedians, are more introverted and less emotional. Where Comedians are driven by having fun and attaining social recognition, Sidekicks are driven by the need for security, stability, and belonging. Sidekicks need to see how they fit into the inner workings of a franchise and what role they will play. Resistant to change, they make slow, informed, and emotionally agonizing decisions about whether or not to start a business. Having a natural tendency to "play not to lose" rather than "playing to win," they seek to eliminate risk and miss opportunities in the process. They are known to be highly detailed, organized, slow-paced, and patient. Having the gift of objectivity, they can see both sides of an issue. They are the best listeners and the easiest to get along with of all the four characters. Since they are introverted and prefer a predictable environment, they are often seen as timid, possessive, risk-averse, and resistant to change.

Your Value in Business

You are very objective and can see all sides of an issue. You make level-headed and carefully thought-out business decisions.

You are very methodical and process-driven. No one has probably ever accused you of being a rebel. You will spend more time memorizing a franchisor's operations manual than trying to rewrite it, which most franchisors will welcome.

You function well within a structured environment. You will follow the franchise system as it was written.

You have great listening skills and a good memory.

You are empathetic. People like you.

You are a team player and an excellent team builder. Members of your team see their own value.

You are a communicator. You keep others in the loop.

You are a servant leader. Customers will go away satisfied and happy.

You are easy to talk to and relate to.

You are highly analytical and will study the numbers and performance criteria of a business.

You are very persistent and consistent. Once you tap into the "winning hand" of a business, you will play that hand again and again, without getting bored or feeling like you have to change it.

You know how to build quality relationships with your customers, employees, and the franchisor.

You have strong customer skills or aptitudes. Being good at soliciting feedback, you will listen to your customers' needs.

You are a "steady Eddie," and your business will function with precision.

What Will Kill You If You Aren't Careful

You struggle with multi-tasking. You like to do one thing at a time and complete tasks before you start the next one. Unfortunately, small businesses are typically not linear and new stuff happens every day. You have to be able to change your daily action plan on the fly, which doesn't play to your strengths.

You experience a high degree of fear of the unknown. Fear can sometimes paralyze you. You have to learn how to walk with fear as a companion much in the same way a recovering alcoholic walks with urges to drink but doesn't act on them. You will need to learn not to make fear mean anything or allow it to stop you from plowing forward.

You have high security and stability needs and are uncomfortable with ambiguity. In business, you will face many ambiguous moments requiring you to assume more risk than you are comfortable facing.

You need time alone to decompress. You may find it hard to decompress.

You prefer a slow-paced environment. The goal in business however, is to create a fast-paced environment where the cash register is ringing constantly.

You can be overly persistent and possessive. You have to learn that there are times to cut and run.

You are quiet and diplomatic. With most franchisors, the squeaky wheel gets the grease. If you aren't receiving the support you need, you will have to overcome your natural tendency to avoid a conflict and either get loud and angry like an Action Hero or get up on your soap box and preach like the Comedian. Franchisors, of course, don't like this, but many franchisees do this because it works.

Your Ideal Franchise ...

Is a stable business and not prone to dramatic swings due to seasonality, the economy, or other conditions outside your control.

Sells products or services, which are necessities rather than luxuries and are stable rather than trendy. Some examples include house cleaning and dry cleaning.

Plays into your customer service strengths, like specialty retail.

Is a repeat customer business, allowing you to build rock-solid relationships, like hair care.

Allows you to pace your day like automotive care, and isn't prone to customer rushes, like flower shops on Valentine's Day.

Has an established and identifiable brand. Let's face it, you aren't a promoter. You are more comfortable behind the counter than outside on the sidewalk. Look for a business where the Comedians and Action Heroes have already built the brand and you do what you do best; maintaining the brand's integrity.

Has an outstanding reputation for maintaining excellent franchisee-franchisor relations. You enjoy being a member of a high-performance team.

Generates fewer transactions but those are high ticket/high margins. You may not multi-task well or fare well in a fast-paced environment. You need a "tortoise business" where slow and steady wins the race.

Creates happy customers. You may not enjoy a business such as transmission repair where many customers feel like they're being ripped off. You would do better with a business like ice cream where everyone is smiling all of the time.

Is either advertising or location driven, meaning your customers come to you. You aren't exactly the type who will wear holes in your shoes from beating the streets doing cold calling.

You Are a Private Eye If ...

You are precise, exact, focused, detailed, neat, systematic, polite, logical, professional, open-minded, and slow-paced. You are the most analytical, compliant, and methodical of the four characters. Private Eyes are driven by an internal need for perfection and want clear instructions about what's expected of them. Their motto is "Tell me how you want it done and I'll do it." They are very task-oriented and once they are clear about what's expected, they become very self-directed. Unlike Action Heroes who seek control over others, they prefer to work alone. They pride themselves on being informed, pouring through information, and analyzing data prior to making any type of decision. Because Private Eyes are introverted and prefer to work alone, they can be seen as aloof, critical, and antisocial. Private Eyes need more details and information than the other three characters before being able to make a decision. Thus, they can also be seen as missing the big picture, fearful, risk-averse, and resistant to change.

Your Value in Business

You are objective and open to new information.

You are very methodical and process-driven.

You are quality-driven. Your customers will be amazed at your level of conscientiousness and pride of service. They will have a hard time finding a business that cares about each transaction the way you do.

You function well within a structured environment. You will follow the franchise system, even if you aren't in total agreement with the structure or system. You adapt well. No one has probably ever said about you, "You know that (insert your name), he/she is always bucking the system!"

You have great listening skills and you remember details. You are a genius with detail. You categorize everything like the library's Dewey Decimal System and know where everything is.

You seem to know everything about everything. And what you don't know, you know where to go to find out.

You will find holes in any system, and have the uncanny ability to spot what is missing. You are brilliant at creating processes and procedures that plug these holes.

You are diplomatic. You walk and speak softly.

You are highly analytical and an Einstein with numbers.

You are very persistent, consistent, and people can count on you to do what you say you are going to do by when you said you were going to do it.

You work at a steady pace and are self-directed.

You gather information and make data-based decisions.

What Will Kill You If You Aren't Careful

You will struggle with many of the same issues as the Faithful Sidekick, so refer back to their list.

You prefer to be alone. Your ideal franchise business would be "lighthouse keeper," but they don't have one. Being alone means *you are the business*. If you aren't working, you aren't getting paid. And when you are working delivering a product or service, it means you aren't marketing for new customers. By your nature, you resist building a team.

You also struggle with multi-tasking. You like to do one thing at a time and complete tasks before you start the next one. As we said with the Sidekick, small businesses are typically not linear and new stuff happens all the time. You have to be able to change your daily action plan on the fly, which doesn't play to your strengths.

You struggle with fear. You have to learn how to walk with fear as a companion much in the same way a recovering alcoholic walks with urges to drink but doesn't act on them. You will need to learn not to make fear mean anything or allow it to stop you from plowing forward.

You need time alone to download. You may find it hard to download during the day.

You can get so caught up in the details, you miss the big picture. You can lose sight of what the details add up to or what they mean.

Because you are a perfectionist, **you can spend too much time on a given transaction.** You need to learn what is "good enough to satisfy the customer" rather than always trying to achieve inner perfection. Once you have the quality required to satisfy the customer, move on. It's better to achieve high volume and excellence than low volume and perfection.

You may be seen as aloof, antisocial, and difficult to do business with.

Your Ideal Franchise ...

Is highly structured and systematic. All you need to do is execute.

Is advertising-driven, not direct sales-driven. Let's face it. You aren't going to cold call. You need a business where customers are finding you through advertising, the Internet, or the Yellow Pages.

Has few or no employees. You prefer to work alone.

Has limited customer interface. As long as you get the job done well, on time and on budget, that's enough. You aren't the one who's going to schmooze your customers at the bar during Happy Hour.

Gives you the down time you need to decompress and allows you to mentally prepare for each customer interface.

Differentiates from their competitors by the quality of products and services it offers. You are meticulous and quality-driven. Make this work for you.

Tracks and offers easy access to all key performance indicators. You manage by analysis and need the data to analyze.

Specializes in one product or service. You pride yourself as an expert, not a generalist. Find a franchise that is well known for one particular product or service.

Is technical in nature. You are a technical genius, make it work for you.

Has fewer transactions, but they're high-ticket ones and offer high margins. You are built for comfort, not for speed.

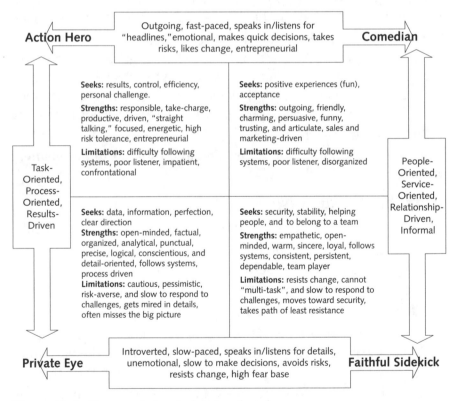

Figure 3-1. Summarizing behavioral styles

What Character Do You Play?

We described these typecast actors as if people were all one character and none of the others. While most people tend to act according to one dominant style, they typically will exhibit the characteristics of two styles. Also, people's style will vary in intensity from individual to individual. Chances are when you read the descriptions, you found at least one character you completely identify with and another that you sometimes do and sometimes don't. You probably also identified one or more characters with whom you regularly have conflicts. For instance, Faithful Sidekicks and Action Heroes struggle to get along. Private Eyes and Comedians also have difficulty in relating to each other. When you study style differences you will typically discover two things:

1. People whose typecast actors are different than ours have skill sets (or a particular genius) we don't have. If you start a franchise it's wise to surround yourself with different actors who possess different skills and have a different take on the business. They will contribute to you in ways you cannot begin to imagine.
2. We are too busy conflicting with or judging others whose style is different than ours. We don't appreciate their gifts and get around to bringing them on our team. As a result, we mostly hire and surround ourselves with people just like us, killing diversity and limiting possibilities.

When interacting with the same characters as their own dominant character, Action Heroes, Comedians, Faithful Sidekicks, or Private Eyes can communicate effectively. However, communication breakdowns occur when one character converses with a *different* kind of character. Let's look at an example.

Imagine that we're in an office and about to watch an Action Hero department head interact with a Faithful Sidekick subordinate. Let's assume the Action Hero has just returned from a meeting with his vice president to discuss reorganizing his department.

The Faithful Sidekick, who seeks a stable environment and likes to prepare mentally for change, asks "What happened during the meeting?" and listens for the details about what was discussed. Being an Action Hero, however, the manager doesn't offer any details, just "headlines." The Action Hero responds, "We talked about some changes in our department."

Because the Faithful Sidekick doesn't receive the details he was listening for, he begins probing by asking more questions, such as "What types of changes?"; "Who will be impacted?"; "What are you hoping to achieve?"; "When will changes occur?"; "What do we need to do to prepare?"

The Action Hero, who likes to control conversations and has difficulty listening to or explaining details, becomes frustrated with the Faithful Sidekick, and feels like he is being bombarded by quesitons. Since the Action Hero is quick to exhibit impatience, he snaps and says, "Don't worry about it. When I'm ready to announce it, I'll announce it!"

The Faithful Sidekick, who seeks stability, security, and belonging, then thinks, "My Stupid, Hotheaded Boss Just Singled Me Out and Put Me Down!"

Because the Faithful Sidekick usually shrinks from conflict instead of addressing it head on, he doesn't go back to his manager to let him know how he was offended. Instead, he waits for the Action Hero to recognize his improper treatment and apologize.

But because the Action Hero is more task-oriented than people-oriented, he's oblivious to the fact that a personal issue now exists with the Sidekick, and never resolves it. The Sidekick, who values relationships, remains dumbfounded as to why the Action Hero never apologized for his outburst. Rather than confronting his manager, he harbors a grudge and gossips about the Action Hero to other employees, creating a disruption in the office.

Both parties share a profound negative experience because neither party was responsible for the impact of their typecast actor on the other.

If the Action Hero understood the needs of the Faithful Sidekick, he would have taken the time to explain the necessity for change and given the Sidekick ample opportunity to ask questions and acclimate.

If the Faithful Sidekick understood the needs of the Action Hero, he would have made an appointment to speak to the Action Hero, set an agenda for that conversation, and prepared the Action Hero in advance with the Sidekick's concerns and the types of questions he would ask during that meeting. The Sidekick would also have had a direct conversation with the Action Hero explaining how he was offended by his outburst and not expect the Action Hero to already know that. Since Action Heroes are very responsible people, the Sidekick would have then received the apology he wanted and the situation would be resolved.

What if ...

The Action Hero built a powerful relationship with the Sidekick and regularly consulted him to hear both sides of issues, to check out opinions against facts, to get feedback on issues involving how to approach different types of people, and other areas where the Action Hero is weak. How much more effective would the Action Hero be with the Sidekick's help and support?

The key to effectively communicate with any of these characters is to understand and speak inside of their individual communication styles. The key to performance is to know your characters' genius and weaknesses. Align your genius to what's required to succeed in any given franchise and compensate for your weaknesses by hiring different characters. Respect and celebrate these differences and you build a high-performance team.

How Can I Predict Others' Styles?

You can predict someone's style with a high degree of accuracy by asking yourself two basic questions.

Question One: Does this person appear outgoing, emotional, and expressive or introverted, distant, and reserved?

- If they appear more outgoing, emotional, and expressive, then you know that your candidate is either an Action Hero or a Comedian.
- If they appear more introverted and reserved, then you know that your candidate is either a Private Eye or a Faithful Sidekick.

If your candidate is outgoing, emotional, and expressive, then ask:

Question Two: Is the candidate informal and friendly or professional and businesslike?

- If the candidate is professional and businesslike, you're probably dealing with an Action Hero.
- If the candidate is more informal and friendly, you're probably dealing with a Comedian.

If you find the person you are speaking to is more introverted, you can stop there. Faithful Sidekicks and Private Eyes have similar gifts so making the distinction is not important. Since roughly 80 percent of introverts are measured to be sidekicks, just asssume the person is a Faithful Sidekick.

In Summary

There are no "right" or "wrong" styles; styles just are. However, people believe that their style is right and other styles are less effective, which is why, left to their own resources, franchisees will hire employees just like them. This diminishes their ability to build a high-performance team, decreases their results, and increases their risk.

Consider there are no right or wrong styles for franchising in general, *but there are right and wrong styles* for individual franchise opportunities. As you investigate franchises, you will see that top performers have similar styles to other top performers and underperformers have a tendency to exhibit similar styles as other underperformers. One predictor of how you will perform in any given franchise system is to determine how people just like you perform. You will have a high probability of achieving similar results.

Chapter 4

What Does Winning Look Like?

Home from another long business trip, Ken dragged himself out of the car, pulled his suitcase out of the trunk, fiddled through his pockets to find his house keys, and opened the door to his home. "Home at last," he thought. As he walked into his kitchen, his two-year-old son stared at him in horror. Terrified of "the stranger" who unexpectedly "broke into" his home, Ken's son ran and hid behind his mother for safety. In that moment Ken made a bold decision. "I will not be a stranger to my children." With that decision, Ken was one step closer to owning a franchise. Months later, Ken was a franchisee of a home-based consulting business.

Remember how Zig Ziglar said, "People don't buy drills, they buy holes"? Ziglar asserts that people don't want the tool; they want the results. Carrying that point forward, it's our opinion that people don't buy franchises, they invest in a desired future. Ken didn't want a business. Ken wanted to be a dad. His franchise was the drill. Before you even think about a franchise, you must ask yourself, "What am I drilling for?"

In his landmark book *The 7 Habits of Highly Effective People,* Stephen Covey saw that before highly effective people engage in activities, they create a clear vision of their desired outcome. Their tasks and conversations are then designed to bring about that vision.

It makes sense. Would you consider hiring a remodeling contractor who tells you he doesn't work from a set of blueprints or drawings and just wings it? His crew just shows up one day, rips down some walls, hammers nails into boards, and sees what happens from there.

Of course you wouldn't. Yet isn't this exactly how most people live and work? We engage in so many conversations and feverish activities that we lose sight of what we want to accomplish. We forget to pause to see if we are heading toward our desired destination.

Franchising is all about producing results and creating a desired future. Investing in a franchise gives you an opportunity for deep personal and career transformation, allowing you to put the past in the past and create something new with your life and work.

When franchisees are *not* producing great results, the culprit is usually one of two things: they don't have specific goals, or they have goals but don't allocate enough (or any) time to achieving them. By learning effective goal-setting and time-management techniques now, you can prevent most performance issues from arising in the future. Goal setting and time management are essential building blocks of successful franchising.

Goal Setting and Benchmarks

Before you research any franchises, you should set three- and five-year goals. Goals must be both financial and "quality of life" (or non-financial) in nature. Financial goals should take into account cash flow, savings, net worth, equity build-up, and spendable income. Quality of life goals should consider lifestyle issues that are important to you, like having dinner at home three nights a week, being able to take vacations, attend soccer games, make a difference in the community, and so on. Don't overlook quality of life goals or you're setting yourself up for dissatisfaction. Quality of life goals are more important than financial goals. Why? Because many people who invest in a franchise have already made a decent living in the past. Aside from earning a paycheck however, they couldn't find a compelling reason to go to work in the morning. Money alone was not enough to keep them going, and money will not hold your interest long either. While you will have some minimum threshold of earnings which you won't dare to venture below, once that threshold is exceeded, you will find that your quality of life then becomes the driver.

Virtually all franchisors have key performance criteria that help you and the franchisor determine whether or not your business is winning. You will be taught how to track sales, labor costs, cost of sales, and other statistical measures. Franchisors design their business and support systems to help you structure your business to achieve these measures and monitor results. However, we know of no franchisor who measures and tracks how many meals you've eaten with your children or how many of the kids' soccer games you've attended. Franchisors measure your success by their definition, not yours. Most franchisors have no clue as to whether or not their "successful" franchisees are living the life they originally desired when they invested in the franchise. Franchisors follow the money. And as we've already stated, money won't hold your interest for long.

Additionally, in order to secure SBA loans, bank financing, financial support from your family, or other forms of financing, chances are you will need to write and submit a business plan or cash flow projections to the parties from whom you're seeking financing. In your plan you will detail the tactics and strategies you will execute to drive the sales, contain the costs, maximize the cash flow of your business, and repay your loan. To succeed in business, you have to generate money.

Imagine that you're in business, money is tight, and you are two months late on your loan payments. The loan officer calls you to see what happened. You tell the loan officer that while you don't have the money to pay the two installments, you did attend all your kid's soccer games this month. Most likely the loan officer will sarcastically reply, "Congratulations. I'm nominating you for father or mother of the year. Where is my money?"

Like the bank, the franchisor also wants its money on time. Franchisors, like banks, are as focused on achieving their own financial goals as you are in achieving your complete and total definition of success. We're not saying this is right or wrong, it's just the way it is. If you were to list and prioritize the many reasons you're looking to start a franchise, where does "Helping the franchisor exceed its corporate objectives" show up on your list? So you want yours, the franchisor wants theirs, the bank wants theirs, and the world turns.

It's solely your responsibility to create a clear definition of the financial and quality of life goals that define what winning looks like for you. Use your definition of winning as your criteria to compare various franchise opportunities. The franchise where you have the highest probability of attaining both your financial and quality of life goals is the franchise you make an investment in.

It's easy to lose sight of your goals. Prospective franchisees often get caught up in their perceptions of the problems and challenges of the business rather than whether or not the franchise can help them achieve their objectives with a high degree of probability.

For instance, you may be investigating a residential home-cleaning business and from talking to franchisees you hear there is high employee turnover. Afraid that you may get stuck cleaning houses you think, "My momma didn't send me to college so I can clean toilets and vacuum carpets." Your knee-jerk reaction is to dismiss the opportunity. However, whether or not there's employee turnover isn't the real issue at hand. Given employee turnover, your focal point should be whether or not you can still achieve your goals with a high degree of probability. Therefore, goal-focused prospective franchisees will dig deeper and ask such questions as:

- What are the franchisor's hiring and retention strategies?
- What is the impact of turnover on the business?
- How long does it take to find replacement help?
- What training programs are in place to train replacement labor?
- How long does it take a new hire to become productive?

Every franchise has its unique challenges to overcome. Franchisors either have proven systems and a demonstrated track record for overcoming these challenges or they don't. Dismiss those who don't. Investigate those who do by asking questions like the ones above. The most important part of your investigation is to thoroughly interview and visit many existing franchisees. We will show you how in detail in Chapter 9.

Goals Schmoals! Why Should I Care about Goals?

In his book *What They Don't Teach You at Harvard Business School*, Mark McCormack tells of a Harvard study conducted between 1979 and 1989. In 1979, the graduates of the MBA program were asked, "Have you set clear, written goals for your future and made plans to accomplish them?" Only 3 percent of the graduates had written goals and plans. Thirteen percent had goals, but had not put them in writing. And 84 percent had no specific goals at all.

Ten years later, in 1989, the researchers found that the 13 percent of graduates who had non-written goals were earning twice as much as the 84 percent who had no goals at all. And most surprisingly, they found that the 3 percent of graduates who had clear, written goals when they left Harvard were earning, on average, *10 times as much as the other 97 percent of graduates all together!*

Keep in mind, there are no dummies at Harvard, so students' intelligence level was a constant, not a variable in this study. The variable was whether or not clear, written goals were set with plans to accomplish them.

Clear goals, whether financial or quality of life in nature, must pass the S.M.A.R.T. test.

Specific

Goals need to be clearly articulated and written down. "Making a lot of money" is not specific. Making $200,000 is specific. "Having more control over time" is not specific. "Going to ten of my son's Little League games and ten of my daughter's dance recitals this year" is specific.

Measurable

You have to be able to create a tracking system; a method of keeping score. This lets you know whether or not you are on track and whether you've hit your goals. If your goal is to make $200,000 by the end of the year, on June 30th you should have earned $100,000 or you may not be on track. On December 31st, you either hit your income goals or you haven't. It isn't open to opinion or speculation.

Using the previous example, if you attend eleven Little League games, you won. If you only went to six, you fell short. It isn't open to interpretation or opinion.

Attainable

Goals must be considered both possible and worthwhile pursuits, or you won't be motivated to achieve them. For instance, you may say your goal is to make $1 million a year, but if you have never made more than $100,000 a year, you may not really see this goal as possible and not take aggressive steps toward achieving it. As a franchisee you may want to experience a 20 percent increase in sales, but if you think it's going to take working 90 to 100 hours a week to achieve that goal, you may not consider it a worthwhile pursuit. And you won't be motivated to hit this goal.

Realistic Timetable

Goals have to have a deadline, a "by when" date. Goals without a deadline don't inspire commitment. It's human nature not to take action on anything you wish to achieve someday. Think of how long you have thought about starting a franchise. Have you set a deadline as to when you will open? If not, other more urgent activities will take precedent and your dream will be pushed further and further back.

If you don't have a deadline as to when you are going to start, then you may have a good intention, but you don't have a plan or a goal. A wise man once said, "The road to hell is paved with good intentions." Good intentions don't make a difference, committed action does. You will never be called forward into committed action without a specific, measurable, attainable, and time-limited goal that's worthy of being achieved. Activities with deadlines attached to them grab your attention and create a sense of urgency and action. For instance, you know you have to get your taxes done by April 15th. If your goal is to get your taxes done on time, April 14th will be a very productive day for you!

Goals with deadlines that are too far out also don't inspire action. Think about something in your life that you wish will occur within the next 20 years. Are you taking action now? Think about when you bought your home. Did you think, "Here is where I'm going to live for the next 30 years!" or did you think, "This home is ideal for now." You aren't wired to think more than three to seven years out. Goals with extended timelines are as useless as goals that you want to achieve "someday" because they don't inspire action. With franchising, consider setting long-term goals with a three- to five-year time limit.

Making Your Desired Future S.M.A.R.T.

Go back to the worksheet in Chapter 2, titled "Creating a Desired Future." You were challenged to identify and prioritize your "must haves" and "want to haves" in your life and career. Now is the time to tie down your desires and make a commitment.

S.M.A.R.T. Goals

My "Must Haves" (highest-priority objectives and absolute necessities)	By when do you commit to achieving this?
My "Wish to Haves" (high-priority objectives but not necessities)	By when do you commit to achieving this?

By assigning short deadlines as to when you will achieve your goals and objectives, you immediately create urgency. Urgency creates action and commitment. Action and commitment generate results.

Street Smart Franchising

As a franchisee, it still isn't enough to have S.M.A.R.T. goals. Goals should be broken down into monthly, weekly, and daily targets.

Thinking about annual or even monthly goals can be intimidating for many franchisees. A franchisee's day moves fast and furiously. Sometimes it's hard for franchisees to carve out enough time to think beyond one day.

But when their goals are broken down into daily chunks, even the biggest annual goals seem doable. Business appears less daunting when they work a daily plan for attaining daily targets. Franchisees who approach business this way have the luxury of working one day at a time without having to look too far into the future. They go into the day knowing that their daily targets are aimed at attaining their monthly benchmarks; their monthly benchmarks are focused on attaining their year-end goals; and their year-end goals are aligned with attaining their three- to five-year goals. So by attaining today's targets, they are attaining their three- to five-year goals. All they need to do is wake up and do it again.

For instance, a franchisee may have a goal of increasing sales $50,000 this year by increasing its customer base. If the franchisee assumes each customer is worth $100, then the franchisee must find 500 new customers this year. On the surface, this appears to be a daunting task. However, when looked at on a weekly basis, the franchisee must find about 10 new customers. When broken into daily chunks (assuming a Monday-through-Friday type of business), the franchisee must find two customers per business day. When split into daily targets, suddenly the $50,000 increase doesn't seem as daunting or unattainable. The franchisee is left empowered to design activities to bring two more customers in the door or make the phone ring two additional times. Once the second customer calls or walks in, the franchisee has achieved the objective. If they choose, they can stop for the day and focus on something else. Tomorrow, all they need to do is to wake up and do it again.

Many people, as they investigate starting a franchise, look out and see all the things that have to happen just to get started. Then they look further ahead and see all the things that need to happen to become successful. They become intimidated by what appears to be an impossible, Herculean task.

How Do You Eat an Elephant?

Taken as a whole, a big goal can appear to be impossible, just as eating an entire elephant in one bite would seem impossible. Big goals need to be approached one bite at a time. If you keep taking one bite at a time, eventually the elephant disappears. You will look back wondering where the elephant went. It's the same with franchising.

A great franchisor understands that, left to your own resources, you will try to eat the elephant of business success all in one bite and choke. They present the goals in bite-sized pieces and feed you one bite at a time. If you get too far ahead of yourself worrying about such things as, "What about the ears? What about the legs? What about the trunk? What about ... " They will say to you, "SHHHHH-HHHHHHHHHHH, it's not polite to talk with your mouth full. After you swallow what's in your mouth, take another bite."

Weak, unskilled, and unsophisticated franchisors will just show you the whole elephant and hand you their version of a knife, fork, and bib. "Have a go at it!" they say. "You have my number. Call me if you choke." A franchisor whose only value to their franchisees is that from time to time they perform the Heimlich maneuver and dislodge elephant chunks isn't earning their franchisee fees or royalties.

Effective Time Management

Chances are, at some time in your life, you have taken a time management class, read about time management in books, and learned to use either an electronic- or paper-based day planner to organize, prioritize, and schedule your day. "Why, with this knowledge, and these gadgets," you ask yourself, "do I still feel like I can't get everything done I need to?"

The answer is simple. Everything you ever learned about managing time is a complete *waste of time* because it doesn't work.

You have bought into time-management gadgets and systems the same way other poor souls have been suckered into buying worthless swamp land in Florida or toll bridges in New York. We aren't saying time management gurus are dishonest people who are out to take your money. They are noble men and women who, no doubt, seek to make a difference in the lives of others. But if you were to have an honest conversation with time-management and other self-help gurus you'll find that they don't get everything done either.

So, you are waist-deep in the middle of the muck and mire of a massive time conspiracy which you are just waking up to. The good news is that in this chapter you will learn how to pull yourself out of the swamp.

Before you can even begin to manage time, you must know what time is. It would seem logical that you can't manage something if you don't know it when you see it. So, what is time?

Webster's Dictionary defines time as "the point or period at which things occur." Put simply, time is when stuff happens.

There are two types of time: clock time and real time. In clock time, there are 60 seconds in a minute, 60 minutes in an hour, 24 hours in a day, 365 days in a year, and so forth. All time passes equally. When someone turns 50, they are exactly 50 years old; no more or no less.

In real time, all time is relative. Time flies or drags depending on what you're doing. For instance, two hours at the Motor Vehicle Department feels like twelve years. And yet our 12-year-old children seem to have grown up in only two hours. If you were to ask that same person who just turned 50, "How old you would be if you didn't know how old you are?" chances are you won't hear "50" as a response.

Which time describes the world in which you really live, real time or clock time?

The reason time management gadgets and systems don't work is that these systems are designed to manage clock time. Clock time is irrelevant. You don't live in or even have access to clock time. You live in real time, a world in which all time flies when you're having fun or drags when you're visiting your in-laws. Additionally, real time is mental; it exists between your ears. You create it. *Anything you create, you can manage.* In this chapter we will dispel clock time myths and teach you the seven truths about real time.

The Seven Truths about Real Time

Truth #1: Everything Happens Now

Chances are, you now relate to time as if you are standing in the middle of a timeline.

| Past | Present | Future |

You think you are here facing this direction

You "look back" on the past, like the past is somehow behind you. You "look forward" into the future as if it's in the distance, and you are marching toward it. You relate to the future as if it's a destination, like a city on a map, like it's a place you have to get to.

However …

The past is in the past. It's gone; you will never have that moment back. The past is a spent resource.

The future is an illusion because the future as the future never occurs. Eventually, the future will be now and then it will be past. Every past moment once occurred as a present moment. The future will enter the universe as a present moment. You can't live in either the past or the future. All you have is now. All you ever had was now. All you are going to have is now. All life happens, all work occurs, all results are achieved—now. Whether or not you succeed in franchising is a direct result of how you choose to spend this very moment … and the next moment … and the next moment after that. If you're not taking action now to achieve the life and career you desire, you are designing a future now that assures that this life and career *never occurs*. The timeline is a time lie. Wake up! Stop living and working a lie and start living and working *now*!

Once upon a time there lived a true time-management master named Christine. Christine had not always been a time-management master. Most of her life she struggled to manage clock time just like you. The wife of a key employee of a photo retail franchise, she, like the rest of us, worried about her family's future and spent most of her time engaged in thoughts, activities, and conversations which, looking back on it, really didn't matter. One day, Christine had to go to the hospital to have a routine gall bladder operation. After the operation, the surgeon informed her that although her gall bladder operation was a success, in the process he discovered that she had cancer. The cancer had advanced, attacking and destroying most of her major internal organs. There was nothing more that the doctor could do. He projected that Christine had about two more years to live.

After a period of brokenhearted shock, Christine quickly regrouped, committing to do the most with the little time she had left. She spoke simply and directly for miscommunication wasted time. She spoke openly and honestly, for pretense wasted time. She loved and forgave, for judging and resenting wasted time. Rather than wallow in self-pity, Christine invested time in being present to the simple joy of being alive.

Christine did not invest her time brooding over what her life could have been. Instead she lived moment to moment, accepting and making the most out of what was.

Because Christine was so accepting of her disease, someone once asked her, "What's it like for you to wake up every morning knowing that you are so close to death?"

Without thinking she lovingly responded to that person by asking another question, "What's it like for you to wake up every morning pretending that you aren't?"

Christine went on to say that when she finally accepted and embraced death, she experienced life. She saw life as a priceless and precious gift that other people were afraid to open. She possessed a screaming desire to tell people to rip open the box and enjoy what's inside. She said that when she tried to get that message across to people, they didn't seem to get it.

Make sure you aren't one of them.

Consider for a second that your life is like a basketball game. You are standing on the court and your game clock is ticking. God is the timekeeper and He will not stop the game clock. At some point the buzzer will sound and your game will be over. Take a look around and see how others are playing their game.

Some people play as if they are frozen; they hold the ball and are afraid to shoot. Others pass the ball, hoping someone else will shoot the ball for them. Still others simply sit on the bench, either living inside the empty promise of "I'll get into the game someday," or waiting for their clock to run out with no expectation of ever playing.

Make sure that none of these will be you.

Don't waste your life watching the clock tick or pretending there is no clock. Don't hold the ball or pass the ball off to anyone else. Certainly don't sit on the bench, waiting for someone to give you permission to play your game.

This is your game to win or lose, so take a shot.

Franchisees Take a Shot

As their ball soars through the air toward their intended target, they experience the fullness of their life and work. Others hold the ball, pass the ball off, sit on the bench, or take their ball and go home. They experience a sort of death by compromise.

Consider that your game has only two certainties. The first certainty is that you will miss 100 percent of the shots you don't take. The second is that your game will end. If you were going to take a shot with your life and career, what would that shot be?

Consider that if you take that shot, you must learn to live with risk. If you hold or pass the ball, you must learn to live with regret. If you sit on the bench or take your ball and go home, you must learn to live with apathy.

Of risk, regret, and apathy, which do you choose to live with? Christine chose risk. By doing so, she reaped a mental and emotional wellness that far exceeded the limitations of her physical illness.

If you choose a career in franchising, you are choosing a life with risk ... delicious, exciting, nerve-racking, nail-biting, life-altering, "I can't wait to see what today brings" kind of risk. Risk, while certainly scary, may be, however, the least scary of all the available options in the end.

Take a moment and fast forward to the end of your game, the end of your life. Consider a life in which you never took your shot. Will you have peace or regret?

Truth #2: We Fill "Now" with Three Things

There are only three ways to spend time: thoughts, conversations, and actions. Regardless of the franchise system you choose, the system will be comprised of three things: thoughts, conversations, and actions. A masterful franchisor is one who has taken the time to identify and document all the thoughts, conversations, and actions a franchisee must be engaged in to win. Additionally, these franchisors know how to give these thoughts, conversations, and actions away to new franchisees, eventually helping them think, speak, and act expertly for themselves. Let's look at thoughts, conversations, and actions individually.

Thoughts. What do peak-performing franchisees think about? How do they view their businesses? What do they think about their customers? How do they relate to their products or services? Suppliers? Other franchisees? The franchisor's support staff? Themselves? Their future? Winners have similar thoughts to other winners. Underperformers also think alike. If you identify the mindset of a winner and make their mindset your mindset, you are positioning yourself to win.

Conversations. What conversations do winning franchisees need to be engaged in? Who should they be talking to? About what? What should they be listening for? What needs to happen as a result of those conversations? Peak-performing franchisees have conversations that matter with customers, employees, and other people who can further their business.

Sales calls, for instance, are a conversation. Management and delegating are also primarily done in the form of conversation. Regardless of the franchise system, most top-performing franchisees are excellent communicators. They may not all be charismatic, but they all know how to listen with understanding and how to be understood. They know the high-priority conversations that drive the business, for example, sales conversations. Underperforming franchisees waste time engaged in meaningless conversations with people who don't impact their business or about topics which don't make a difference to the business. When you investigate franchises, find out who those high-priority conversations are with and what they're about in each system you consider.

If you don't consider yourself a good communicator, consider that great communicators were not born great communicators. Up to the age of two, they all said, "goo-goo, da-da, bah-bah" and a host of other nonsense syllables. Great communication requires great training. Nonprofit organizations such as Toastmasters and for-profit companies like Dale Carnegie (a franchised company) offer training to help you build your skills.

Actions. What do peak performers do that average or underperformers don't do? What are the high-priority activities that drive results? What are a winner's habits? Find out how peak performers spend their day and replicate it in your business. Peak-performing franchisees know what the leverage points of their business are and spend their time focused on the key activities which drive all results. Underperforming franchisees get mired in the minutiae of the business and trap themselves by doing busy work, which doesn't have a major impact on results.

Consider that all actions and conversations have one thing in common: they all originated in thought. Thoughts drive conversations and actions, which means thought is the most important of the three ways to spend time because it generates the other two. We're not saying you should climb to the top of a mountain, sit in a lotus position, stay there all day, and expect to be successful. However, we are saying you will never speak and act like a winner within a particular franchise until you learn how to think like a winner.

Most franchisors will only train you in how their winners speak and act. The majority of franchisors won't train you to think how their winners think. Most simply don't know how important that piece is. Once you've completed the franchisor's training programs, you probably will only have a little more than two-thirds of the franchisor's total winning formula. Most likely, you will be left to your own resources to put that missing critical-thinking piece in place. But putting this piece in place will be less difficult than you think. All you need to do is to ask a winner, "What do you think about your customers? What do you think about your products and services? What do you think about when you plan your day? What do you think about your employees? What do you think about (fill in the blank)?" Then choose to think like they do.

If you learn how to think like a peak-performing franchisee you will instinctively speak and act like a peak-performing franchisee. It's that simple.

Truth #3: It's Never Finished

When is the last time you went to bed saying, "I got everything done. There's nothing left to do. I will now enter the restful sleep of a fully completed day"?

What do the Loch Ness Monster, the Easter Bunny, and fully completed days have in common? There are no such things.

It's a given that there is simply not enough time to finish everything you'd like to do each day. And who says you have to? Is there some local ordinance that requires you to get everything done? Are you subject to fines or imprisonment if you don't? As we already stated, no one gets everything done every day, especially time-management gurus. Do you know what Thomas Jefferson, Albert Einstein, Thomas Edison, Abraham Lincoln, John F. Kennedy, Ghandi, and Mother Teresa all have in common? None of them got it all done either.

Part of being human is to have stuff on your to-do list at the end of every day. As a franchisee you aren't going to get it all done either. But you do need to get the important things done. You need to identify and complete those high-priority activities which generate all the results.

Once, a small business owner was complaining that his sales were flat and he was overwhelmed with all the moving parts of his business. Taking an inventory of everything he did during the course of the day, he saw he had accomplished at least 15 things a day, sometimes more, but always at least 15 things. His biggest challenge was he always had *25 things* on his to-do list. But most of what he accomplished had little or nothing to do with generating sales.

Not wanting to work 24 hours a day to accomplish the 25 things on his list, he decided to work smarter. When he finally accepted the fact that he will go into every day accomplishing only 15 things without pretending he could do more, he regained his focus. Before he started every day he identified at least 8 high-priority activities to generate. By only planning eight instead of 15, he realistically left time for employee and customer interruptions. He learned how to prioritize and delegate the low-priority activities that were consuming him. He regained his passion for his business and starting driving results.

Truth #4: You Waste Time

As we already stated, most of what you do, say, think about, and worry about, doesn't matter. That sounds harsh, but it's accurate. Famed management consultant Dr. Joseph Juran studied what executives did everyday. He found that 20 percent of an executive's activities, thoughts, and conversations produced more than 80 percent of the person's results. What's more, he found this premise held true across people and across industries. This principle also applies to franchising. Acknowledging similar research by Italian economist Vilfredo Pareto, Juran named his concept "The Pareto Principle" which is also known as the "80/20 Rule."

According to Juran's hypothesis, only 20 percent of your current activities produce 80 percent of your total results. And 80 percent of your time is typically spent generating less than 20 percent of your results. Put another way, 80 percent of all time is wasted on thoughts, conversations, and activities that don't make much of a difference.

If you buy this concept, then it becomes obvious that if you become a franchisee you should identify and master those "20 percent thoughts," and have more "20 percent conversations," and more "20 percent activities." In his book *The 7 Habits of Highly Effective People*, Dr. Stephen Covey stated effective people make a distinction between what is urgent and what is important, and then focus on the important. For instance, answering a ringing telephone may seem urgent, but unless the franchisee knows a customer is on the other end of the line, the conversation may have no measurable impact on the financial health of the business. What if the franchisee picks up the phone and finds a telemarketer who is selling vinyl siding? The conversation becomes one of the 80 percent of the activities that waste a franchisee's precious time and take away from time dedicated to driving results. Compare that to handling a customer complaint in such a powerful way that the complaining customer now becomes a lifetime customer. Both may take the same amount of time, but each produces materially different results.

Regardless of the franchise you investigate, it will have a version of the 80/20 rule. There are a small number of thoughts, conversations, and actions which drive the entire business and seemingly a million thoughts, conversations, and actions that a franchisee will get sucked into, which chew up time and don't make a difference. Each is identifiable. Keep this in mind as you research different franchises. One strategy is to keep a simple chart.

How Do You Get This Information?

The 20% thoughts, conversations, and activities that produce more than 80% of a franchisee's results	The 80% thoughts, conversations, and activities that produce less than 20% of a franchisee's results
What are the 20% thoughts?	What are the 80% thoughts?
What are the 20% conversations?	What are the 80% conversations?
What are the 20% actions?	What are the 80% actions?

When we address franchisees during national conferences, seminars, or workshops, we like to ask them the following questions.

1. Given where you're spending your time right now, assuming you change nothing, in three years …

    a. How much money will you be making?

    b. Will you hit your financial goals?

2. If you spend 50 percent of your time focused on the "20 percent that produces 80 percent of the results," in three years ...
   a. How much money will you be making?
   b. Will you be working more/the same number/or fewer hours?
   c. What would you do with the extra time/money?

3. If you spend 80 percent of your time focused on the "20 percent that produces 80 percent of the results," in three years ...
   a. How much money will you be making?
   b. Will you be working more/same/or fewer hours?
   c. What would you do with the extra time/money?

This is an empowering exercise for a franchisee to complete. Franchisees get to say how much time they put in and where it's spent. If you become a franchisee, you will too. You can spend your moments strategizing about how to take your business to new levels, executing brilliant conversations, and being engaged in focused activities, or building expert business skills. You also can waste time a million different ways and accomplish very little. Every franchisee's future results are a function of the skill and quality of a franchisee's and franchisor's thoughts, conversations, and actions taken now. And a franchisee's current results are a direct function of the skill and quality of a franchisee's and franchisor's thoughts, conversations, and actions taken in the past.

Franchisees get to say what they did then and what they do now. Therefore every franchisee is responsible for their own results and the author of their own life and business. And their results are not random. Results are a function of what they are doing right now.

Truth #5: There Is No Such Thing as Multi-tasking

Have you ever tried to have a conversation with someone who you knew had their mind on something else? How did that make you feel? Was it a powerful and productive conversation or did you have the experience you were merely being tolerated? Did you get the results you were looking for or were you left dissatisfied?

Conversely, did you ever have a conversation with someone who gave you the experience that you were the most important person in the world right then and the entire outside world would have to wait for a moment? How did that make you feel?

Who would you rather do business with?

What separates the first person from the second? Is it their communication skills or is it their singular focus?

Another way people deceive themselves is by believing they can multi-task. Computers multi-task. People are only wired to hold one thought at a time. The person in the first conversation heard about multi-tasking and bought that thought hook, line, and sinker. The person in the second conversation knows the truth and sees multi-tasking as a version of being distracted while pretending to be efficient. If you are to be a peak-performing franchisee you must:

- Choose to be in the conversation you are in.
- Be present to the thought or activity you are currently engaged in.

You can practice the skills it takes to become a peak-performing franchisee right now, long before you make an investment. Practice doing one thing at a time. Master being in one conversation at a time.

Most franchisors rely on their franchisees to provide excellent customer service in order to create an advantage over their competition. When customers shop a franchise, they know they aren't far removed from the owner and ultimate decision maker. If they have a question or an issue, they will expect your attention. They won't like it if you multi-task. Would you?

Practice paying attention to people. Focus on the task at hand and push other thoughts out of your mind. This type of listening or focus requires energy and practice. Eventually you build that muscle and listening and focus become easier and easier.

Your brain will focus on the task at hand only when you are working from a daily plan, with your conversations and tasks mapped out for the day. Otherwise you will come in and out of what you're doing, trying not to forget things or let things fall through the cracks. Peak-performing franchisees prepare a written time plan in the morning and then let the paper remember while they work their plan. They plan on spending at least 50 percent of their day on the 20 percent of activities and conversations that produce 80 percent of the results.

Truth #6: You Determine Your Future Now (Or, Why Didn't I Do This Sooner?)

Your future is determined by the quality of your thoughts, actions, and conversations, done now. The future is not random. It's a simple function of the quality and results of the thoughts, actions, and conversations you have every day.

When a franchisee rigorously watches what they think, say, and do and builds upon the skills with which they think, say, and do, they know exactly what their future holds. Their success is not random. Success and failure are functions of how franchisees choose to spend this moment and the next.

Think about how long you've been dreaming about starting a business. You have the inkling, but then you fill "now" up with other thoughts and activities, designing and creating some other future than the one you profess you want. When people who are thinking about starting a franchise give up on their dream they usually blame the timing. "It's not the right time," they say. They desire more freedom and control, but only if external events are aligned to give it to them. Where is the freedom and control in that?

The people who start franchises are generally not faced with any fewer pressures, commitments, or obligations than those who never pursue franchising. But they understand that all they have is now. "If I don't do this now," they think, "then perhaps I never will." They make a decision that this *is* the right time because they accept the responsibility for making it the right time.

Starting a franchise is much like starting a family. Originally, you want to have a nest egg, have a stable job and home, and be positioned to give your children a great life. However, as time passes, the nest egg never seems big enough, the job never seems secure enough, and so on. You realize that perhaps there is no right time. Eventually you just throw your hands up in the air and say, "I can always find an excuse not to have children. We will find a way to make it OK." And then you start a family. You took responsibility for making it the right time, even in the face of not knowing how to do it. Somehow, you survived and things turned out OK. You look back and wonder why you waited so long.

It's the same in business. If you start a franchise, you most likely will have to take responsibility for making now the right time. The stars typically don't align. Good timing generally doesn't randomly create itself. You can always create reasons, either real or imagined, which you will use to convince yourself this isn't the right time. Then you will most likely fill up your day with activities designed to make sure tomorrow isn't the right time either. Then one day, you will look back on your life and say, "What happened? Where did my life and dreams go?" Or you can start new today. You take matters into your hands and declare today is the right time because this is your life and you have a say in the matter. Like having children, you may not know how everything is going to work out. And like having children, you will most likely survive and look back one day and say, "Why didn't I do this sooner?"

Truth #7: Nothing Happens Exactly as Planned. Plan on It!

Think about the last time you planned an event. You covered every detail, you planned for every contingency, you thought of every angle, and then you executed your plan. Then, as the plan unfolded, people, events, and stuff started happening that you didn't plan for. You thought you planned for it all, but somehow things you didn't plan for still found their way into the equation. You adjusted what you were doing, went with the flow, and chances are, although things didn't go as planned, the results were still what they needed to be. Management expert Tom Peters once said he felt much time spent on planning was overrated as nothing seems to go as planned. It either goes better or worse.

We aren't saying you shouldn't do your due diligence, develop a business plan, or create a cash flow analysis before you invest in a franchise. All these exercises are critical to developing a thorough understanding of the franchise you chose. We are saying your planning should allow for things not going as planned.

As a franchisee you will frequently be interrupted and pulled in different directions. While you cannot eliminate interruptions, you do get to say how much time you will spend on them.

You can practice the following techniques now which will position you to win as a franchisee in the future.

- Any activity or conversation that is important to your success should have a time assigned to it. To-do lists get longer and longer to the point where they are unworkable. Appointment books work. Schedule appointments with yourself and create time blocks for the high-priority thoughts, conversations, and actions. Schedule when they will begin and end. Have the discipline to keep these appointments.
- Know how long these important thoughts, conversations, and actions take. Then design them into your day.
- Schedule time for interruptions. Plan time to be pulled away.
- Consider carrying around a schedule and recording all your thoughts, conversations, and activities for a week. This will help you understand how much you can get done in the course of a day and where your precious moments are going. You'll see how much time is actually spent producing results and how much time is wasted on unproductive thoughts, conversations, and actions.
- Plan to spend at least 50 percent of your time engaged in the thoughts, activities, and conversations that produce most of your results.
- Take the first 30 minutes of every day to plan your day. Don't start your day until you complete your time plan.
- Also, take five minutes *before* every call and task to decide what results you want to attain. This will help you know what success looks like before you start. And it will also slow time down. Take five minutes *after* each call and activity to determine whether or not your desired result was achieved. If not, what was missing? How do you put what's missing into your next call or activity?
- Put up a "Do Not Disturb" sign when you absolutely have to get work done.
- Schedule a time to answer e-mail. Practice not responding to e-mail just because it came in, unless you are in a business where immediate response is a competitive advantage.
- Practice not answering the phone just because it's ringing, unless you are in a business where human response is a competitive advantage.

- Disconnect instant messaging. Don't instantly give people your attention.
- Remember that it's impossible to get everything done. Also remember that chances are 20 percent of your thoughts, conversations, and activities produce 80 percent of your results. Since most of what's left undone is a waste of time anyway, who cares? Get the important things done first.

Chapter 5

What Does It Take to Win as a Franchisee?

s you research different franchise opportunities you are faced with the difficult task of answering five questions with great clarity:

1. What are the key ingredients in the franchisor's recipe for success?
2. Which of the key ingredients do I possess?
3. Which of the key ingredients am I missing?
4. What is the franchisor's track record of helping others like me acquire these missing ingredients?
5. Am I willing to do what it takes to acquire these ingredients?

Answering these questions requires great discernment on your part. As you investigate franchising, you will most likely work with a franchise sales representative (or development representative as they are sometimes called) who may not know all the ingredients needed to succeed in the particular franchise you are examining.

Few have actual experience operating a franchise and therefore have limited or no real-world experience. That doesn't mean their feedback isn't useful and shouldn't be trusted, but it does mean you need to conduct a thorough investigation on your own. Franchise sales representatives will generally know enough about operations to be competent in their roles as ambassadors to people investigating their franchise, but not to the extent where they could train and support new franchisees or run the franchise business competently themselves. This is perfectly acceptable since their role is not to train and support new franchisees or run an operation. While they can explain on a high level what it takes for you to succeed as a franchisee, they may omit, gloss over, or not take into account certain skill sets or habits required for your success. Again, it's your responsibility to conduct a thorough investigation.

Secondly, most franchise salespeople have high integrity and a desire to look out for both your and the franchisor's best interest. They will take an interest in you as a person and will facilitate your investigation process.

But many franchise salespeople don't invest enough time in interviewing and screening you properly to accurately determine both the transferable skills and abilities you possess and those you are missing. If you were to examine the background of franchise salespeople, most are salespeople and approach their positions as a salesperson would. They are "hunters," and you are looking at the business end of their gun. They will push the features and benefits of their franchise and move you toward closure, meaning a "yes" or "no" decision as expediently as possible. The law of averages has proven that the longer you take to move through the process the more likely it is that either fear or a lack of passion will keep you from ever closing the deal. "Time kills deals," is their mantra. Sometimes you'll feel pressured to make a decision before you feel you have conducted a reasonable investigation.

Keep in mind, only one or two out of every 100 people who inquire about a particular franchise actually move forward. The others fall away for reasons we discussed earlier. Franchise salespeople are under enormous time pressure to expeditiously sift through the 100 to find the one or two who will move forward. Earlier we told the story of the vice president of franchise sales of a large national automobile body repair franchise who once said, "It isn't my job to qualify franchise candidates. I will give anyone their God-given right to fail." If your skill sets don't line up with the core competencies required to be successful in the business, some will turn a blind eye and attempt to coerce and manipulate you through their sales process anyway. They aren't concerned with your heightened risk or how financial failure may impact your family. Nor are they concerned with how your failure will impact their customers or their brand. They are more concerned with "closing the deal and getting one on the scoreboard." They are like the slick, used car salesman who once tried to sell a man a used SUV. "Whether or not you purchase this car from me," the salesman said, "I can tell we will become great friends!" A month later (after he did *not* purchase the car from the salesman) the man sarcastically remarked to his family, "Gee, it's been a month and I haven't heard from my new friend yet. That's not like him. I hope he's OK!"

More sophisticated and enlightened franchisors not only look for franchise salespeople who can sell, but those who have the ability, vision, integrity, and discipline to accurately qualify and screen potential franchise buyers. Peak-performing franchisors will employ franchise salespeople who take the time to get to know you and compare your skills and aptitudes against their profile of a successful franchisee. They will communicate what it takes to win and check to make sure you understand them properly. If your skills don't match up, they may not immediately disqualify you from the process. But they will inform you of your weak areas and how those weaknesses may impact your business. They will ask you what training you will take or what you are committed to do to improve in those areas. For instance, you may have weak computer skills. They will inform you that unless you take some computer training, they can't award you a franchise. They may even be ready with some recommendations of good computer classes you can take which will fill in your knowledge and skill gaps. These are the true professionals. Unfortunately, right now they are in the minority. However, they are getting attention within the franchising industry. We expect more and more franchisors to adapt their best practices.

Another problem in franchising is that compensation and bonus structures of a franchise's salespeople are tied to whether or not you join the franchise, not whether or not you perform well once you are open. Their compensation is tied to their ability to move you through the sales process, regardless of whether or not you match the profile of a successful franchisee. Few franchise salespeople have the final say as to whether or not you're approved as a franchisee, so checks and balances do exist. But the problem remains that the compensation of most franchises' salespeople is incongruent with both yours and the franchisor's goals for your personal success within their system.

Professional franchisee recruitment is a hot topic right now with franchisors. More attention is being paid to the long-term benefits for both the franchisor and potential franchisee of recruiting highly qualified franchise candidates and rejecting everyone else. They are also waking up to the negative financial and emotional costs of selling franchises to people who simply aren't positioned to win. This dynamic is changing, but slowly.

This issue will remain until franchisors completely change the way they view their franchise sales departments. Even the words "franchise sales" is a tip-off as to why there's a problem. If you were applying for a key position within the franchisor's company, you'd likely be taken through a series of several hard interviews and interface with human resources. What would you think of working for a company who named their HR department the "Vacant Position Sales Department?" If a franchisor has a key management position open, they interview and screen. They have open and frank discussions with potential management candidates about the responsibilities of the job and what it takes to win. If the candidate is thinking the position isn't right for them, they wish them well and terminate future interviews. They understand the risks of making a bad key management hire and will work hard to find the right person.

Many franchisors don't consider franchisees "key management" and therefore don't put in the time or energy to make sure they are finding the right franchisee partners. Again, they are more keyed into the quantity of franchises sold than the quality of franchisees they award a franchise to.

For a franchisor, "quantity" of franchises sold versus "quality" of the franchisees seem to be opposing forces. Franchisors are pushed and pulled by these forces and struggle to find just the right balance.

This isn't good or bad, it's just the way it is. Most franchise sales-people are high-integrity, knowledgeable salespeople who accepted this position because they have a genuine love of people and want to see others win. They usually aren't compensated if you do or held accountable if you don't.

Expect these salespeople to ask you highly personal questions such as what you have in the way of personal assets to finance a business. While this may put you on edge, it's in your best interest to answer these questions openly and honestly. Since one of the leading causes of business failures is undercapitalization, it's reasonable to ask you such questions and in your best interest to answer them completely and without reservation.

As we discussed in a previous chapter, many franchisors will use tools such as behavior profiles and personality inventories. They will spend the first several meetings and conversations getting to know you and qualifying you, much as if you were interviewing for a senior management position within their organization. Once they are clear that you match their criteria of a successful franchisee, watch the salesmanship begin! A skilled franchise salesperson will know you fit the profile of a successful franchisee before you do. Take their salesmanship as a compliment. They want you!

While the franchisor will help you identify what it takes to win, their feedback will be incomplete for the reasons we discussed earlier. You can count on franchise salespeople to give you a good overview of what it takes, but most just don't know all the details. You'll have to gather your details from other sources. We will show you how in a later chapter.

The KASH Model of Success

As you gather data, you'll find successful franchisees of particular franchise systems have a tendency to think and act alike. They view their customers, employees, business, competition, products and services, and the franchisor the same way. They know the same things, possess similar skill sets, and engage in the same high-priority activities each day. Underperforming franchisees also view their customers, employees, business, competition, products and services, and the franchisor the same way.

The success formula for every franchise opportunity is composed of four key ingredients:

1. Knowledge
2. Attitude
3. Skills
4. Habits

This recipe of success has been coined "KASH," after the first letter in each word. Here's how we define each element:

Knowledge: Peak-performing franchisees have high levels of product, service, and operational knowledge and are students of their business and industry. They know the business model inside and out and execute it consistently over time. They understand the nature, dynamics, and leverage points of their business, meaning they have identified all the activities which produce the greatest results.

Attitude: Franchisees with appropriate attitudes have a realistic and healthy view of their business and the franchisor. Their results may not always be great, but they know why —and are working with the franchisor to continually improve. It's often said that attitude (or thinking), drives all action. Given the same external event (such as a potential conflict), some attitudes, such as "problem-solving," generate greater results than others, such as "fighting." Few franchisees create outstanding results without first generating winning thoughts. Attitude and mental management is one of the keys to achieving peak performance in any franchise system. When franchisees learn how to manage their minds, their bodies follow.

Skills: Skillful franchisees exhibit polished and effective behaviors on the job. They know how to accomplish their jobs and manage their customers and employees with great effectiveness. They possess and refine the skills required to be effective franchisees. They execute their knowledge with freedom and ease.

Habits: Franchisees with good habits produce results easily and naturally. They are almost "unconsciously competent." They tend to produce more results than other franchisees do with the same amount of time, money, and energy. They know what the high-priority activities are that produce the greatest results and spend more time engaged in these activities than do underperforming franchisees.

Remember, KASH elements are very different from each other. For instance:

- Knowledge consists of the "mental maps" that show us what to do and how to do it.
- Writing a service order in an automotive franchise hinges on knowledge of automotive repairs and of the front-desk order system. Skill is the way the service writer uses this knowledge. It's how the person writes up the order and conveys it to the shop mechanics or how the person handles a customer complaint. Knowledge is invisible, but skills are observable. Usually, good skills rest on a foundation of good knowledge. So both elements are equally important.
- Attitude is the lens through which franchisees view the world. It's the meaning they place on events and how they respond to them.

A particular franchisee's business results may be sub-par, especially during the start-up of their business. Rather than blaming the franchisor, responsible franchisees will be more apt to engage in problem-solving. Webster's Dictionary defines "attitude" as a "mental position" or "state of mind." Attitude is often linked with "good" or "bad," but that's not what Webster means. Webster defines "attitude" in terms of how we relate to people or events as we experience them. For example, in the face of a customer complaint, one franchisee's attitude might be: "This customer is the lifeblood of my business." This franchisee will then design a solution congruent with that attitude, hopefully creating a lifetime customer in the process. Another franchisee facing the same complaint might harbor the attitude, "This customer is a pain in the neck." Chances are, the customer will go away dissatisfied and perhaps take other customers with him or her.

Habit is the cement or glue that combines knowledge, skill, and attitude into long-term peak performance. It occurs over time with practice and refinement, and is learned through mistakes and sheer hard work.

Athletes call habit "being in the zone." It's the point at which people produce results almost unconsciously. And franchisees with good, strong habits usually produce more than do franchisees who are still forming habits. Performing at the level of habit is your ultimate goal as a franchisee.

Let's take a look now at the importance of peak-performing franchisees to every franchise system. You'll see that without these stellar performers, the world of franchising might quickly go dark.

The Importance of Peak Performers

The survival of every franchisor lies in their ability to recruit and train peak-performing franchisees. Here's why peak performers are indispensable.

To themselves: The rewards of peak performance are easy to see. First, they receive the obvious rewards of greater revenue, profits, and personal income. Next, they experience the intangible satisfaction that comes from doing a great job. Finally, their strong results tend to confirm the reasons they entered the business in the first place. This encourages them to produce even greater results in the future.

To the franchisor: Peak performers produce the greatest royalties and usually consume the least of the franchisor's time and money. This makes them the financial bedrock of any franchise organization. Because they produce the lion's share of the franchisor's profit margins (remember franchisors rely on royalty collections), they subsidize the support provided to weaker franchisees. Royalties generated by peak-performing franchisees pay management salaries, fund new initiatives, pay the franchisor's rent, and keep the franchisor's lights on. And because these franchisees are so competent, they help the franchisor validate its business model and show other franchisees what it takes to win. Peak performers don't just bring financial advantages. They also help franchisors achieve a competitive edge in the marketplace because they're able to capture a disproportionate share of the market. This makes it difficult for competitors to stake out and hold a position. So, whether you view them from a financial or a marketing perspective, peak-performing franchisees are crucial to a franchisor's success. A franchisor will never succeed unless their franchisees are successful.

To other franchisees: Peak-performing franchisees are seen as leaders within their franchise system. They serve as a constant reminder to other franchisees of what's possible if they stay on course. Many assist the franchisor and other franchisees as mentors and coaches, helping newer or underperforming franchisees discover the success formula for their business.

To customers: Peak-performing franchisees generate higher levels of customer satisfaction and repeat business than do lower-performing ones. That's because customers prefer to deal with people who know what they're doing. And when they find someone who performs well, they tend to stick with that person and generate referrals.

The Costs of Poor Performance

It's a statistical fact of life that for every peak-performing franchisee, there are also average, below average, and failing franchisees. And for every franchisee that under-produces or fails, there's a financial cost and a human cost that affects everyone in the franchise system.

To themselves: Franchisees who fail can, and often do, lose substantial sums of money. If they put their homes up as collateral, some may lose those homes. If they invested all of their savings, they may lose their retirement security and children's education trends. With these losses come stress-related illnesses such as heart attacks and depression—or worse.

To the franchisor: Franchisee failure makes it increasingly difficult for a franchisor to recruit new franchisees and halts forward momentum. Prospective franchisees want to invest in a franchise that's flying high, not crashing and burning. When franchisees fail, the chain doesn't grow and eventually starts to decline. The franchisor will lose its ability to negotiate positive terms with vendors, receive choice locations, favorable financing rates, and hire and retain good employees. Lastly, successful franchisees don't sue. Many failing franchisees may look to recapture some of their lost investment by suing the franchisor. This forces the franchisor to spend money on attorney's fees in order to protect the franchise system rather than on making investments which produce results for the other franchisees.

To other franchisees: Failure also pulls other franchisees down. Franchisees develop a "foxhole" mentality and see fellow franchisees as "brothers-in-arms." It's emotionally devastating for other franchisees to watch one of their own fail. One franchisee's failure can halt forward momentum in an entire market. A failed franchise allows the franchisor's competition to create a beachhead, emboldening them to go after more markets, attacking the livelihood of other franchisees.

To customers: Franchisee failure leaves existing customers doubting the quality of the products and services and the value of the brand. You can almost hear the customer thinking, "If this product or service was any good, they would have made it. I'd better shop their competition."

In short, a franchisee's failure breeds more failure, creating a vicious, downward cycle. But a franchisee's success breeds more success, creating a virtuous upward cycle.

Most franchisees' success or failure isn't random. Success and failure are a direct result of the KASH balance. If a wide gap exists between your personal KASH and the KASH required to succeed in a franchise business, then you're at risk. If your KASH is consistent with the profile of a successful franchisee, then most likely you're in a position to win.

As we discussed, all KASH is acquired. No doctor ever presented a newborn baby to his or her mother proclaiming, "Congratulations, you've just given birth to a future successful automotive repair franchisee."

The KASH Deficit Analysis

Identifying whether or not you will succeed within a particular franchise system requires personal detachment and rigorous self-examination.

- Start with your existing KASH.
- Identify the KASH required to succeed.
- Then subtract the second from the first and you'll know what's missing.

If your KASH deficits are too high going in, you run a higher risk of failure. If your KASH deficit is low, you are a more natural fit for the business. While franchisors have training and ongoing support aimed at building your KASH balance, they aren't miracle workers. If your KASH isn't already in reasonable alignment with a particular franchisor's KASH formula of success, take a pass. There are thousands of different franchise options available. Find one that fits. We will show you where you can go to explore your options later in this book.

Once you have identified your KASH deficits, ask yourself, "Am I willing to do whatever it takes to acquire my missing KASH?" If you are one who works hard to achieve your goals, you will likely work hard to acquire your missing KASH. If you are one who just likes to get by, you'll most likely lose your investment. If you like to coast, or if you simply struggle with learning new things, find a franchise whose KASH formula of success is a mirror overlay to your personal KASH balance. Again, we will show you where you can explore your options in a later chapter.

While you need to develop your own KASH model for each business you explore, we've included a self-assessment tool to help you create a baseline to use when exploring franchises.

Greg Nathan, corporate psychologist, franchising expert, and founder of The Franchise Relationships Institute, helped us develop the following worksheet to use when identifying your starting KASH balance.

Fill out the survey to the best of your ability. Don't over-analyze the questions, just go with your gut and circle the first answer that comes into your head.

My Starting KASH

Name			Date		

Trainability	Always	Sometimes	Never
I adapt well to change	3	2	1
I invest money in my personal development	3	2	1
I am open to feedback on my weaknesses	3	2	1
I am open to trying new ways of doing things	3	2	1
Total for Section			

Marketing/Sales Aptitudes	Always	Sometimes	Never
I am skilled at influencing others with my viewpoints	3	2	1
I am comfortable talking to strangers	3	2	1
I am a creative problem-solver	3	2	1
I am a confident presenter	3	2	1
Total for Section			

Motivation	Always	Sometimes	Never
I have clear goals	3	2	1
I achieve what I set my mind on	3	2	1
I honor my commitments	3	2	1
Faced with a problem I can create a proper solution	3	2	1
Total for Section			

Working with Others	Always	Sometimes	Never
I compromise to comply with the wishes of the majority	3	2	1
I get along well with others	3	2	1
I resolve differences with others without creating arguments	3	2	1
I listen to other viewpoints	3	2	1
Total for Section			

Leadership	Always	Sometimes	Never
I achieve my goals through the efforts of others	3	2	1
I will spend money developing my employees' skills	3	2	1
I positively impact others	3	2	1
I can get a diverse group of people moving together in the same positive direction	3	2	1
Total for Section			

Health	Always	Sometimes	Never
I have high energy	3	2	1
I know how to handle stress	3	2	1
I exercise regularly	3	2	1
I eat properly	3	2	1
Total for Section			

Personal Responsibility	Always	Sometimes	Never
I will use my full-time best efforts to drive the business	3	2	1
I accept responsibility for my results	3	2	1
I accept responsibility for my failures	3	2	1
I accept short-term pain for long-term gain	3	2	1
Total for Section			

Family/Friends Support	Always	Sometimes	Never
My famiy/friends support my decision to start a business	3	2	1
My family/friends understand the risks involved	3	2	1
My family/friends understand the time commitment involved	3	2	1
I have stable, positive relationships with my family/friends	3	2	1
Total for Section			

Systems Orientation	Always	Sometimes	Never
I am comfortable following processes and systems others create	3	2	1
I adjust my methods/habits to comply with existing procedures	3	2	1
I am organized and good with detail	3	2	1
I am willing to comply with systems, even if I am in personal disagreement with the methods	3	2	1
Total for Section			

Entrepreneurial Drive	Always	Sometimes	Never
Even when at first I don't know how, I find a way to make things happen	3	2	1
I take risks	3	2	1
I am comfortable with ambiguity	3	2	1
I multi-task well	3	2	1
Total for Section			

Small Business Acumen	Always	Sometimes	Never
I create and achieve budgets	3	2	1
I use technology	3	2	1
I read financial statements	3	2	1
I create and achieve strategic plans	3	2	1
Total for Section			

Time Management	Always	Sometimes	Never
I use my time wisely	3	2	1
I do high-priority activities first	3	2	1
I create a daily plan and work my daily plan	3	2	1
I guard my time	3	2	1
Total for Section			

Communication Skills	Always	Sometimes	Never
I speak clearly	3	2	1
I say what needs to be said	3	2	1
I listen with understanding	3	2	1
I communicate well in writing	3	2	1
Total for Section			

What Is Your Starting KASH Balance?

You have completed the first step in assessing your KASH. But it's hard for anyone to completely assess themselves. Ask friends, family, and co-workers you trust to also assess you. Compare your answers with theirs and see what you learn. Where you have great disparities, say you rated yourself a "3" and they rated you a "1," discuss their answers with them. In a nonjudgmental manner, ask "How did you come up with that answer?" See yourself through their eyes.

Pay particular attention to any section where you or others rated you a total of "8" or below. You may be at risk in these areas. This doesn't mean you won't succeed in franchising, but it does mean you need to plan on improving your skills in these areas.

Pay attention to the particular line items where you or others rated you a "1." What are you prepared to do to improve yourself in these areas?

Pay attention to particular line items where both you and others rated you as a "3." How can you capitalize on these strengths?

Help Franchisors Help You

When you begin contacting franchisors, consider sending the franchisor's representative a copy of this completed assessment. This will help them identify who you are and whether or not you match the profile of a successful franchisee. This helps protect both you and the franchisor's best interest.

Take Responsibility

This assessment will help you determine your personal KASH balance. We can't overemphasize the importance of completing the survey and having several people close to you also complete it for you. In selecting and running your own business it's vitally important to know yourself. Take responsibility for identifying and shoring up your weak areas. Personal responsibility is key.

Chapter 6

The Learning Curve of a Franchisee:
From the Launch to the Zone

Just as human beings evolve as they enter different stages in life, franchisees also evolve as they enter different stages in business. In fact, franchisees move through five distinct phases in linear order: the Launch, the Grind, Winning, the Zone, and the Goodbye (see Figure 6-1 on the next page). Each stage is marked by changes in franchisees' results and satisfaction levels.

This chapter will help you identify each stage and give you proven strategies to accelerate through the learning curve. It's one of the most important chapters in this book—the one you will reread, mark up, and keep referring to. We will discuss how franchisees' KASH (knowledge, attitude, skills, and habits) fluctuate within each stage. We will also show you how to help the franchisor tailor their support to your specific needs within each stage.

As a franchisee, you will go through emotional fluctuations, from the joy at opening (the Launch); to the frustration of putting forth a huge effort for modest results because of the distressing frequency of your mistakes (the Grind); to satisfaction from succeeding in your business (Winning); to your mastery of the model (the Zone). Figure 6-1 lays out the five stages and shows what happens to franchisees' results and satisfaction in each stage. Pay particular attention to the inverse relationship between franchisees' results and satisfaction in the first two stages of the learning curve.

In this chapter, we answer four important questions.

1. What is the predictable learning curve and lifecycle of my franchise and what happens during each stage?
2. What are the three modes a franchisor will use to support me?
3. How do I accelerate through the learning curve toward the Zone?
4. What is the proper combination of franchisor support that will help me accelerate through each stage?

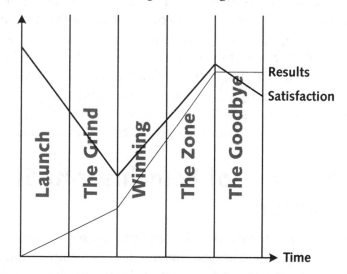

Figure 6-1. The performance/satisfaction curve of a franchisee

Let's look at the Launch from the franchisor's perspective. As we discussed, many franchisors make little or no money from their franchise fee. Franchise fees usually cover the cost of running the franchisee recruitment department. Your franchise fee was probably spent on salaries, recruitment advertising, benefits, supplies, and other departmental expenses for the purpose of trying to find you!

Most franchisors rely completely on the royalty income (and product sales for those franchisors who are also suppliers to their franchisees) for the survival of their businesses. Peak-performing franchisees pay the highest royalties and purchase the most products and thus drive the most revenue for the franchisor. Additionally, because peak performers fully realize the success formula (KASH) of the business, they also consume fewer resources than their counterparts. They pay the most and consume the least, making them (in business terms) the franchisor's highest-margin customers.

Franchisees in the Launch and the Grind stages understandably generate the lowest royalty revenue and product sales for the franchisor because they're still ramping up. If they're being adequately supported, they also consume most of the franchisor's time and management resources. Looking at the franchisor's profitability on a per franchisee basis, many franchisors lose money on franchisees until they grasp the KASH success formula. Established franchisees (those who are in Winning or the Zone) subsidize the ongoing support and training of new franchisees. The success of a franchisor depends on their ability to give franchisees the necessary KASH as quickly as possible. If mature (in business three years or more) franchisees aren't winning, then the whole franchise system may implode. Before we dissect the five stages of the learning curve, let's look at the three ways franchisors give their KASH to franchisees.

Three Modes of Franchisor KASH Distribution

The three ways franchisors will help you accelerate through the learning curve of your business are training, consulting, and coaching. When used in combination and at the right point in your business lifecycle, these modes will work together to achieve the same goal: your peak performance.

Some franchisors instinctively support their franchisees correctly. They may train, consult, and coach their franchisees at the right time and in the right combination without even knowing the difference or what to call it. Others understand the differences and the timing, and have a proven system for supporting franchisees. A third group, consisting of unskilled franchisors, doesn't know the differences or the timing and may never bother to learn. Let's take a moment and identify these three modes just in case you are unfortunate enough to align yourself with an unskilled franchisor. If you are left alone to acquire your KASH, you will at least know what you need, when you need it, and where to look. Additionally, many unskilled franchisors want to do the right thing; they just don't know what the right thing is. If you know, you can train them to provide what you need to succeed.

Franchisor Support Mode One: Training

Training is about teaching you *how* to perform. It's about conveying the knowledge you need; modeling the skills (behaviors) required; and providing opportunities to practice, refine, and lock in what you learned (habits). Here's what differentiates training from consulting and coaching:

- Training involves teaching you "how to fish." The first step is to describe a fish. Franchisee training should be highly structured and remedial, assuming franchisees know little. Many franchisors will send remedial information ahead for franchisees to digest before they come into the franchisor's training program. Don't be offended by franchisors who design remedial programs for franchisees, offering knowledge you already possess. It's much better for a franchisor to assume you know nothing and offer you everything than to assume you know something and leave you with gaps in critical knowledge and skills.
- In training, the assumption is that the trainer knows more than those being trained. The "trainer knows—you don't" dynamic creates a hierarchical relationship between you and the trainer. This isn't a bad thing, just the dynamic of the trainer/trainee relationship. Training is an acceptable forum for a franchisor to "talk down" to their franchisees.
- When you are being trained, communication typically flows down from the trainer to you. Very little flows up, and very little should flow up. For example, picture being in a franchise training class where a new franchisee says, "In our CPA firm, we didn't do it your way; we did it (such and such) way ..." and the trainer responds sweetly, "That probably works great

in a CPA firm, but we're learning how to run a muffler shop, not an accounting practice. Do it our way. Thank you for sharing." You are there to acquire, not offer knowledge. It's time to put much of your past in the past.

- When in a training mode, the franchisor assumes a much more directive role. Expect them to do much more speaking and showing than listening.

- When in training, the franchisor will focus intently on building knowledge and skills, while providing lots of opportunities for you to build winning habits. The mantra of a trainer is "learn, learn, learn, practice, practice, practice!" Remember, practice does not make perfect, practice makes permanent. Only perfect practice makes perfect. Make sure you only do business with a franchisor who regularly monitors your practice, making sure you engage in perfect practice designed to create permanent winning habits.

- Trainers often mistakenly assume that if they show franchisees what to do and how to do it, they will do it unaided in the future. There's often a gap between what people know and what they do. Again, a skilled trainer will monitor your practice and close that gap!

- Skilled franchisors will develop your business and technical skills. Remember, you aren't joining a franchise to learn how to do such tasks as unclog a drain; you're joining a franchise to learn how to make money and create your desired lifestyle by unclogging drains. You need to learn how to deliver the product and market, manage, and promote a business. Only do business with a franchisor who understands that your business skills are as important as your technical skills.

- Just as franchisees don't need to re-invent the wheel, neither does a franchisor. Smart franchisors often use outside vendors to deliver certain components of their training program and adapt their franchise systems to the vendors' products and training. For instance, Dale Carnegie® or Sandler Sales Institute® (both franchises) offer excellent sales training programs which would be difficult to improve upon. Don't be surprised if a franchisor requests or even requires you take outside training programs.

Again, the goal of training is to transfer knowledge and skills. This can be hampered by several common mistakes.

1. Systems aren't properly documented, leaving knowledge gaps.
2. Training programs are "data dumps," offering too much information in too little time.
3. Knowledge is offered but modeling skills are not. David Sandler, founder of Sandler Sales Institute® often said, "You can't teach a kid to ride a bicycle in a seminar." Nor can you teach the skill in a classroom or with a book. Kids get balance by falling down a lot and scraping their elbows and knees. During the "getting balance" process, a responsible parent is right there, ready to offer coaching, hugs, and bandages. Then, unpredictably, almost magically, the kid gets it. He may wobble, but he doesn't fall. He may narrowly miss trees and mailboxes, but he doesn't hit them. The frustration of falling is replaced with the thrill of the ride, a sense of winning, and an empowered feeling called "balance."

   So, too, with franchising. You can't predict when a kid will find his or her balance especially if you're the kid. Getting balance over time however *is* predictable. The kid gets it when they get it and it's pointless to force the issue. Again, so it is with franchising. Franchisees get KASH when they get it. Although a franchisor can't predict when franchisees will acquire KASH, a franchisor should have a demonstrated track record which shows franchisees get it eventually, before they run out of the other kind of cash.

4. More emphasis is placed on training than on consulting and coaching. Knowledge is overrated. For instance, why do so many people smoke? Don't they know it causes cancer? Why are so many adults obese? Don't they know how to order a salad and exercise on a treadmill? Knowledge, on its own, doesn't make a difference. Franchisees' consistent and skillful implementation of their knowledge is what produces great results. Many franchisors assume that if franchisees know what to do, they'll do it. They forget that even with peak performers, there's a great divide between what's known and what's implemented. Skilled franchisors hold franchisees accountable for closing the gap.

Franchisor Support Mode Two: Consulting

Consulting is about fixing problems. After initial training, competent franchisors continue to consult with their franchisees, identifying and eliminating obstacles to growth. While the same person may provide initial training and ongoing consulting, consulting and training are materially different modes of support and are used at different times in the learning curve to produce different results. We will discuss why and when each is used later in this chapter. For now, let's just distinguish the differences. Consulting differs from training in the following ways: In consulting mode, the support person's job is to throw you a fish, not teach you how to fish. They help you fix problems fast, not to increase your knowledge base. The franchisor takes the responsibility of identifying your problems and crafting a solution. Your role as a franchisee is to execute the solution. Often franchisors will train franchisees after the fact; helping franchisees learn how and why a breakdown occurred and showing them ways to prevent a future breakdown. This is ideal because it will also help the franchisees get a deeper understanding of both the unique dynamics of their business; what does and doesn't work, and why.

- With consulting, as with training, communications flows down.
- When a franchisor's support staff is in consulting mode, they take an even more directive role than when they're training. They will probably tell you to "do this and that," but they may or may not get into the rationale behind the directives.

Franchisor Support Mode Three: Coaching

Coaching is about pure execution. Coaching assumes you know what to do and now it's time to get it done. In the face of inaction, coaching is also about discovering why franchisees aren't doing what they already know how to do or using readily available solutions. Here's what differentiates coaching from training and consulting:

- When the franchisor's support staff is in coaching mode, they address situations in which a franchisee knows what to do, but isn't doing it or doing it effectively. They hold franchisees accountable for implementing what they've learned and crafting their own solutions. They also hold franchisees account-able for waking up early and "getting some fish in the boat," because they already know how to fish.

- When coaching, franchisor support staff operates in partner-ship with franchisees. There is no hierarchy. The coach's job is to coach. The franchisees' job is to execute. Each has clear roles and responsibilities.
- In coaching mode, the franchisor's staff focuses on driving franchisees' results. And if results are already good, they drive them higher.
- When there's a breakdown in performance, the coach will immediately start asking questions about what happened, instead of telling franchisees what to do like a consultant or trainer. The coach assumes franchisees have the solution inside them, waiting to come out. By asking the right ques-tions, the coach will assist franchisees in diagnosing their own problems and creating and implementing their own solutions. In the process, franchisees will put in structures or safeguards that will prevent the same problem from occurring again.

> **In coaching, the solution resides with the franchisee, not with the coach.**

Coaching places greater emphasis on asking questions, goal set-ting, action planning, implementation of the plan, and accountabil-ity than do the other two modes. It places relatively little focus on knowledge/skill acquisition or technical solutions, because coaching assumes franchisees already possess the knowledge and skills. All that's missing is proper implementation.

How do these modes differ? Let's assume a franchisee isn't grow-ing their sales as budgeted.

Franchisee: "My sales are off this month …"

The Trainer	The Consultant	The Coach
"Let's hold a sales training program for your salespeople." The problem is identified as a lack of training. It's assumed if the salespeople knew more, they would perform better. **The solution resides with the trainer.**	"Let me follow your salespeople around and hear what they are doing wrong and figure out a solution." The consultant assumes the salespeople or franchisee cannot identify the problem or craft a solution. **The solution resides with the consultant.**	The coach asks, "How many calls are you making? What are customers telling you as to their reasons for not buying? What changed from last month? What do you need to be doing differently?" The coach assumes that by prompting the franchisee with questions, the salespeople or franchisee will identify their own problem and create their own solution. **The solution resides with the franchisee.**

The trainer, if all he knew was training, would jump right into a training solution, assuming that if the franchisee knew what to do, he or she would do it and achieve results. The consultant, if all she knew were consulting, would try to identify and fix the problems herself, many times bypassing franchisees in the process. This is a good short-term fix, but it doesn't empower franchisees to identify and craft solutions for themselves. Aside from disempowering franchisees, this will lead to more dependence on the franchisor in the future. The coach, if all he knew was coaching, would help franchisees identify and resolve their own problems, assuming there's a gap between what they know and how they implement this knowledge. The coach helps the franchisee bridge their own gap. "The system works," the coach says, "now where are you not working the system? What do you need to do to get back on track?"

The point is: if you are to be successful, the franchisor needs to be prepared to mix and match training, consulting, and coaching at the right times. Your role as a franchisee is to internalize the training, and execute the consulting and coaching as it's offered. Let's look at how to successfully navigate the learning curve. (Review Figure 6-1.)

The Launch

When a franchisee signs their franchise agreement, they are filled with mixed emotions. While there's some fear of the unknown, they are mostly filled with a sense of joy and empowerment. It's as if they can look out across the learning curve and see the life they are designing for themselves and their families as if it's already occurring. They know they just took the necessary step to make it happen. This "knowing" fills them with a juicy sense of wonder and awe. Still excited, they move feverishly through the start-up activities such as setting up a corporation, securing financing, finding and securing a location, purchasing opening inventory, and so on. They hang on to the training instructor's every word during initial training. They leave training charged up and ready to make their mark.

Eventually the franchise opens and they wake up every morning ready to take on the day. They eagerly serve customers and treat themselves and their employees gently, seeing rookie mistakes as productive learning opportunities. While money is tight, they have prepared for it to be tight, and they are right on plan.

But because they aren't yet skilled at what they do and customers may not know the brand, their results are poor, as poor as they will ever be. Despite the weak initial results associated with starting a business, they recognize this is temporary and they give themselves permission to learn. They know they will eventually achieve results if they diligently do what it takes to learn the franchise's success formula.

In this and the previous chapter, we harp on the KASH model of success—knowledge, attitude, skills, and habits. Successful franchisees seem to usually possess the same KASH as other successful franchisees in the same franchise system. Unsuccessful or underperforming franchisees seem to reflect the same KASH as their counterparts. Many underperforming franchisees become arrested in their KASH development, never acquiring the necessary skills to successfully navigate the learning curve into peak performance. In this chapter you'll see how your KASH will fluctuate during each stage of your franchisee evolution, and learn what it takes to successfully graduate into the next stage.

Knowledge

When you launch your franchise, much of your past business knowledge becomes irrelevant. Truth be known, when you sign your franchise agreements and write the check for the franchise fee you've invested in the right to be incompetent. What you don't know about your new business could fill an encyclopedia. But you're confident that this knowledge exists within the franchisor and franchisee community and is properly documented. You're confident in both the franchisor's ability to teach you their system and your ability to learn it. You go through the franchisor's training program and so much knowledge is crammed into your cranium you're afraid your eyes will pop out.

Attitude

Life is good. The grass looks a little greener, the sky a little more blue, and birds are singing. Each day is filled with excitement, adventure, and awe. For the first time in a long time, you feel as if you are being called forward into action. Instead of throwing shoes and curses at your alarm clock, you often wake up before it rings, charged up with the electricity of an exciting new day. You are on fire. Work becomes play. In addition to attitude changes, you may experience physical changes. Although you may be sleeping less, you appear rested and relaxed. While your business may not yet be making money, you experience a sense of peace. People may even begin remarking on how much younger or fitter you look. They also complain about your frequent gleeful whistling of *Zippity Doo-Dah* and the theme song from *The Andy Griffith Show* while they're trying to work. For the first time in a long time, your life and career are working together in balance and harmony.

Skills

Let's face it. You will probably stink. This isn't a bad thing, because as we've already discussed, you know you have invested in the privilege of being incompetent for a short period of time. The launch is a time of unconscious incompetence, meaning that you don't know what you don't know. And because you've given yourself permission to learn, you aren't upset about it. Like a famous motivational speaker once said, "Anything worth doing is worth being lousy at for a little while." Unless you are one of those rare prodigies or your background closely matches the skills required to succeed in your new venture, your skills at best will be unrefined. Some skills will transfer over from your past career and some won't. The Launch is a time for deep personal development.

Be mindful that franchisors are typically skilled at imparting knowledge to their franchisees, but often ignore their skill development. You might be left on your own to develop your skills.

For instance, in most franchise businesses, successfully selling your product or service is critical to the success of your business. A franchisor may have documented and taught you the steps of the sale, the benefits of the product or service, and the differentiating factors between your products and services and those of your competition. However, they may have no program to develop your sales skills.

Sales are typically done in the form of oral communication. Put another way, sales is a conversation and good salespeople are expert communicators. Expert communication requires such refined personal skills as:

- **Interviewing skills.** The ability to ask pertinent questions to determine another's needs.
- **Problem-solving skills.** The ability to correctly identify needs and problems and craft effective solutions.
- **Empathetic listening skills.** The ability to put yourself where the customer is standing and see their needs from their perspective.
- **Speaking and being understood.** Being able to relate information to a customer in a way that is relevant to the customer's needs.

While you will find many franchisors who have correctly documented their sales processes, you'll find few franchisors with the ability to correctly identify your missing personal skill sets and with programs in place to fill in your skill gaps. For example, we don't know of any franchisors who have training programs that teach franchisees how to listen. If you have deficits in this area, you're likely going to be left on your own to develop that skill. The good news is that there are plenty of outside courses and training programs that can help you develop specific skill sets. Make sure you have correctly identified which skills sets are necessary to succeed in a particular business as you investigate the business. Take a personal inventory and identify which of those skill sets you possess and which ones you're missing. Budget money, perhaps even several thousand dollars, to invest in programs and training to fill in your skill gaps.

Habits

The second you open your doors, your habits will start to form. At the beginning of the Launch, you have few good or bad habits. But during the Launch you'll either begin the good habit of spending more time executing the high-priority activities, which generate the most results, or formulate the bad habit of wasting time on busywork which produces few results. Carefully document and observe where you spend your time. A key habit to develop during the Launch is to *budget time for learning and skill development.* How quickly you develop your knowledge and skills will determine how quickly you ramp up your business and generate positive cash flow.

Strategies for a Successful Launch

More Training

Training isn't a one- or two-week event that occurs after you sign your agreement, but rather an ongoing process, continuing well past the grand opening of your business. Remember, many franchisors' training programs are a massive data dump, the training equivalent of trying to take a sip of water from a fire hose. Initial training programs are typically done in the vacuum of a classroom setting. You will have little real-world experience. If the franchisor doesn't offer continuing training three- to six-months after you open your doors, ask to take the initial training program a second time, even if this means paying additional fees. Once you're in the real world executing the business model, you develop the context you didn't have in the initial training program. By attending additional training you'll get the franchise training program on a much deeper and more meaningful level.

Not all franchisors offer meaningful training programs beyond their initial classroom instruction before you open. Depending on the complexity of their business model, they should have a three-month to one-year training, skill development, coaching, and mentoring program designed to accelerate you through the learning curve to reach competent levels of performance. Not all do, so beware. Most likely, beyond an introductory point, you will be forced to train and develop yourself, taking total ownership of much of your learning curve. While the world is full of self-taught musicians, artists, and businesspeople, attending music, art, or business schools would make learning faster and easier. But beyond some entry-level, initial training, many franchisors might not offer you additional opportunities. Most franchisors have regular regional and national conferences, which do offer additional training programs, networking opportunities, and panel discussions. However, these forums may or may not address your specific business needs at the time you need it. And these conferences, while valuable, dump more data. Most offer little opportunity for role-playing, skill development, or additional on-the-job training.

When you launch your business, don't focus on profitability. Focus on learning. Identify and acquire the KASH necessary to survive and then thrive.

You'll know you have completed the Launch when you start becoming frustrated and disillusioned with the learning curve. Put another way, your attitude goes in the tank. Instead of whistling *Zippity Doo Dah*, you now hum B.B. King's classic, *The Thrill is Gone*. Don't despair. The thrill isn't really gone; it just hides for a little while.

The Grind

Think about the last time you picked up a new hobby, for example, golf. Adults who picked up golf later in life are thrilled with the decision to learn the game. They got fitted with clubs and shoes, went to the driving range, signed up with a teaching pro, and learned the basics. Some were so giddy, they even bought silly hats, bright sweaters, and loud, striped pants. Learning was fun, and at first they didn't take mistakes so seriously. They let themselves hit pop ups, ground balls, and take Texas-sized divots out of the grass. Hitting into the woods, trap, or lake, although not desired, was really no big deal, it was a given part of the learning process.

Then something happened. Somewhere in the learning process, golf stopped being fun. In fact, it became infuriating to the point that when a golfer's ball splashed into the lake, the offending golf club, or perhaps the entire bag, was flung into the lake right behind it. The permission they had given themselves to make mistakes was revoked and replaced by a demand for results equal to the money, effort, anguish, and loud, striped pants they'd invested in.

The golfer, like the entrepreneur, insists on a proper return on their investment. The golfer has entered into the Grind.

Golf, once explained in terms of heavenly virtue, is now described in a steady stream of hellish obscenities. The golfer, once in awe of everything that is right with golf—the beauty of the course, the peace of the surroundings, and the camaraderie of their peers — now focuses on everything that's wrong with their swing.

From your vantage point as an objective third party who is watching this golfer, ask yourself the following question. Has the game of golf really changed or has *the golfer's relationship to the game* changed?

Now put yourself in the golf shoes of the golfer, experiencing what the golfer experiences. Has the game changed?

This phenomenon also occurs in franchising. In the eyes of the franchisee, the game changes.

If you take an objective look at golf, the game probably wasn't as good as the golfer originally made it out to be, nor as bad as it seems to be now. As a matter of fact, golf isn't good or bad. Golf is what the golfer makes out of it.

It's the same with franchising. As franchisees move through the learning curve, they change their relationship to their business. They revoke their own learning privileges and demand a return on their investment. Work is no longer play. Work becomes hard, frustrating, and excruciating. The glee of Launch disappears. The frustration of the Grind now occupies that space.

As you read this, check your experience. Chances are, just like franchisees mired in the Grind, you're relating to the pain and frustration of the Grind as a bad thing. We invite you into a new, more powerful perception.

The Grind is a good thing! The Grind is a sign of progress, because after the Grind comes Winning. You can't jump from the Launch to Winning without experiencing some Grind.

Some franchisees in the Grind may feel they've halted their forward momentum. Others may even experience failure. These experiences can't be trusted. Just like the game of golf doesn't change as the golfer moves through the sport's learning curve, the game of franchising doesn't change either.

Once, a franchisee of a business service franchisor became visibly distraught during the franchisor's initial training program. Picking up on this, the astute trainer took the franchisee aside during the next break to check in and see what was happening. The franchisee confided, "I'm upset because I know the other franchisees are getting the business quicker than I am. I'm behind the rest of the class."

The trainer gave the franchisee a reassuring smile. "Do you think that when you leave here, you're going to know everything you need to know to become successful or do you think your real training begins when you leave here?"

"I know I'll have a ton of work to do when we leave here," replied the franchisee.

"Will you do what it takes?" asked the trainer.

"Absolutely!" declared the franchisee.

The trainer paused to choose his next words carefully. "Consider for a second," he said, "that not only are you *not* behind the rest of the class, *I'm secretly declaring you the valedictorian!* Everyone else is relishing in the joy of their start-up. You've already moved into the frustration of the learning curve. Congratulations. You're at the head of the class."

The trainer knew that pain meant progress.

Consider for a second that there are two types of pain. The first is like headache pain. We relate to this pain as if it's something bad, something that shouldn't be. We then do whatever it takes to make this pain go away.

However, there's also a second type of pain, like exercise pain. During exercise, muscle burn or fatigue becomes a desired result. We take steps to manifest this pain. We invite it into our bodies. "No pain, no gain!" we say. We relate to exercise pain as a sign of progress, a sign of winning. This pain is good.

For whatever reason, a franchisee experiences the pain of the learning curve of a business as headache pain rather than exercise pain.

Earlier we stated that franchisors, even those whose systems produce outstanding results, report that 99 percent of the people who investigate their franchise end up not moving forward. Why? Many prospective franchisees are terrified of the Grind. They relate to it as if it's a permanent state instead of a temporary part of the learning curve. Remember the kid riding the bike? When he is sprawled out on the sidewalk, bleeding from the elbows and knees, what would lead him to believe that in the next ride he will get balance? But then, one magical, unpredictable time, this is what happens. While baby-soft skin may seem preferable to cuts and bruises, you can't get balance without first having the experience of falling down.

The Grind ends with an empowering "Now I get it!" series of experiences. Just like the kid who gets balance when learning to ride a bike, once a franchisee gets the business, they will always get it. The KASH formula becomes part of their identity.

When polled, most franchisees of most franchise systems report that they are winning by their own personal definition of winning. When asked, "Knowing what you know now, would you make the same decision again?" most answer a resounding "Yes!" If most franchisees win (and they do) and most are satisfied with their decision (and they are), then why don't more people invest in franchises?

They are making their pain go away.

It's hard to describe the Grind to anyone who has never experienced it. However, try the following exercise to get a snapshot of what it's like.

Start by crossing your arms. Notice which arm is on top. Leave your arms crossed and notice what you experience. You know this position because you've crossed your arms this way for years. It's natural and easy for you. You don't feel stress or experience any need to make a change. Got it?

Now uncross your arms. Re-cross them, but this time put the opposite arm on top. Chances are, on the first attempt you couldn't even do it. Now that you finally figured out how, leave your arms crossed that way for a few moments. What are you experiencing?

You probably have some deep-seated thought that you're crossing your arms the wrong way. There now appears to be a right way and a wrong way to cross your arms, and you're now crossing them the wrong way. It's so wrong in fact, that it's making you crazy. So crazy, you can't wait to uncross them. Take a second and watch yourself make yourself crazy over something as silly as crossing your arms. Welcome to the Grind.

Comedian Steven Wright once explained it a different way. "Do you remember how you felt when you leaned too far back in your chair, and you think you're going to fall, but suddenly you catch yourself?" he said. "I feel like that all the time."

While Wright may experience living there all the time, we assure you, your stay in the Grind will be temporary. Wright also said he places Scotch Tape® on all his mirrors so he doesn't walk through them into another dimension. Mr. Wright might be dealing with other issues as well.

Going back to your arm-crossing adventure, what if you were to cross your arms that way every day? Would your "I'm crossing my arms the wrong way" experience eventually change? Would you become more comfortable? Over time, isn't it reasonable to assume you'll have the freedom of choice as to which way you cross your arms?

Franchisees eventually get it and the Grind disappears. It's the franchisor's job to accelerate the "getting it" process.

Let's take a look at a franchisee's KASH when in the Grind.

Knowledge

While in the Grind, knowledge is steadily increasing, but gaps still exist. Franchisees are still dependent on the franchisor, because they don't know what they don't know. Where the Launch is a time of unconscious incompetence, meaning franchisees don't know how bad they really are, the Grind is a time of conscious incompetence. They understand how bad they are and how much further they need to go to win. This realization can be disempowering, terrifying, and frustrating.

But fearing the Grind is like fearing the Boogey Man. When a child realizes there's no such thing as the Boogey Man outside of their own imagination, darkness loses its power. When franchisees understand that there's no such thing as the Grind outside their own imaginations, the disempowerment, fear, and frustration of the learning curve dissipates.

Attitude

To quote an overworked cliché, "The bloom is off the rose." Most franchisees are results-oriented and often results simply aren't to the franchisees' satisfaction or expectations. Here's where franchisees and franchisors disconnect.

> **This disconnection occurs when franchisees need their franchisors the most.**

An objective look at results would show a steady increase in the franchisees' performance. Franchisees will typically produce marginally better results week after week, slow and steady. However, franchisees often get caught up in the frustration of the almost super-human effort it takes to produce those results. Most franchisees have been solid producers in the past. Producers like to produce. They have a demonstrated track record of competently and consistently hitting their personal and corporate objectives. Many can't remember the last time they struggled. They forgot how hard they had to work early in their careers. They only remember and still relate to their past mastery. Because they are struggling to achieve the results they achieve, many get sucked into *the false experience of failing* although they may actually be on or ahead of plan!

Franchisors don't measure false experiences, just results. They aren't living inside the franchisees' phantom experiences. Many of the franchisor's support personnel have never owned a business before and don't get what it is to be in the Grind. So they don't offer the emotional support franchisees desperately need to successfully navigate this stage. Many franchisors are reactive. If the numbers don't show a problem, there is no problem. They assume franchisees will call if there is one. Franchisees respond to the Grind generally one of four ways.

1. Fighters fight. These franchisees create monumental problems where either no, or perhaps tiny, problems exist. They seem to

cry wolf every time something doesn't go as planned. They blame the training, products, competition, support, marketing, pricing, and even their customers. They think, "I'm working the system, but the system isn't working." They blame and complain creating a strained relationship with the franchisor's support team at the time they need this team's best efforts. They become like the child who is sprawled out on the sidewalk who kicks their bike yelling, "Stupid bike! If only I bought another stupid bike I wouldn't have fallen!" The franchisor support team responds to their anger with a "What does this ungrateful @%&%#$!#! franchisee want now?" kind of attitude. They become either curt or make efforts to dodge their calls altogether. Because franchisees think the system isn't working, they start changing the system to coincide with what worked in their previous business or career.

These changes often don't work, prolonging the learning curve, miring the franchisee in the Grind, creating more complaints and changes, which in turn creates more Grind. Some franchisees get so caught up in a death spiral they never acquire the necessary KASH and produce marginal results. Others simply get it over time.

If you're the type of person who pushes off responsibility onto others or fights before problem-solving, remember it's probably not the bike. If you've never ridden a bike before, you'll jump on a $2,000 custom-built titanium bike and probably still wipe out. Be gentle with yourself and others. Learn humility and let others contribute to you. Don't kill off the people who are trying to help you. Own your results and learning curve. Trust the learning process and over time you will achieve balance.

2. Overly optimistic franchisees get caught up in false hopes. They hope things will get better, although they have no plan of attack to acquire the necessary KASH to make things better. When the franchisor calls asking, "How are things going?" The franchisee responds, "Just peachy!" They don't dare admit to "negative thinking," although that's where they spend much of their day. A business coach who works with both franchisees and franchisors, says, "Hope is a beautiful thing; never lose hope. However, hope

is a lousy business strategy." Many franchisors aren't going to pick up on when you are operating inside of "false hope without a plan." They're going to assume when you say you are "peachy," you are, indeed, peachy, instead of pretending to be peachy when you're really petrified. If you are prone to false positive thinking, learn how to shoot straight and say what you're really experiencing so the franchisor can offer you support.

3. Overly pessimistic franchisees will have a Chicken Little "the sky is falling" experience. Don't expect franchisors to confuse falling acorns with the collapse of the world as we know it. These franchisees begin expecting failure, and can easily gather the data to support their conclusions. "Just look at my past results!" they say. In a learning curve however, past results are no indication of future failure because every day new franchisees acquire new KASH, which alters the existing state of their business and what they're capable of achieving in the future. Again, they are like the little kid who is sprawled on the sidewalk, who screams "I will never, ever ride this stupid bike!" Remember that one time the child will get it if he continues to give himself (or herself) permission to just keep pedaling.

   Unlike the Launch, where a franchisee can clearly see across the learning curve into the land of milk and honey, in the Grind, the learning curve becomes a blind curve in which franchisees cannot see past the bend. But when the franchisor examines the franchisee's results, they see a steady progression of positive outcomes. Franchisees in the Grind have the tendency to dismiss data and results, preferring instead to believe the sky is really falling. Again, the franchisor will typically miss the franchisee's false failure experience, examining the data according to plan. If you are pessimistic by nature, trust the data and discount your interpretation of it. Give yourself permission to learn, letting others also contribute to you. Commit yourself to the learning process and you will eventually not only ride the stupid bike, but ride it expertly.

4. Emotionally mature and balanced franchisees manage their emotions, don't buy the false experiences, and give themselves permission to learn. They treat themselves and others gently.

Although they aren't crazy about mistakes, they learn their lessons and move on. They know that slamming into pavement is part of learning how to ride a bike and they don't have false expectations otherwise. They know there will be bruises and bleeding and they know they will scab and heal. They remember that the last fall didn't kill them so they'll probably survive the next fall. They don't blame the bicycle, the bicycle manufacturer, the pavement, or the entire biking industry for their choice to learn how to ride a bike. They know they will be fearful. But they know they will survive the fear because they also remember being afraid in the past, and they didn't die from that fear. They know there will be frustration, and their frustration won't be fatal. Well-balanced franchisees will take the business *one day at a time* with a full understanding that whatever happened yesterday is already in the past and can't be changed.

Just as balance seems to find the child who continues to pedal the bike, well-balanced franchisees know success will find them when they commit to acquiring the necessary KASH of the business. They invested in the privilege of getting to say what happens today and for the ability to own their results, whether or not those results meet expectations. For these franchisees, the Grind is a temporary nuisance, not a permanent nightmare. They know it's a mental state that they create. They don't blame others for their Grind. They know that if they just own their thoughts and emotions for one more day, and do what they're supposed to, tomorrow will take care of itself.

Asking what causes the Grind is like asking what causes the Boogey Man. Franchisees make up the Grind the same way children make up the imaginary demon. The Boogey Man isn't good or bad, just a figment of a child's imagination. The Grind isn't good or bad either, just a figment of a franchisee's imagination. Having a conversation about the Grind with a franchisee who currently is in the Grind is like having a conversation with a child who is certain the Boogey Man is under their bed.

Turning the light on, the adult says "Look under the bed. There's no Boogey Man. The Boogey Man is pretend."

"He's real!" the child replies. "The Boogey Man turns invisible when you come in the room!"

Just as the child can always find evidence to believe in the Boogey Man, franchisees can always find evidence to keep them in the Grind.

The Boogey Man is a child's fear of the dark manifested. The Grind is a franchisee's fear of failure manifested. Kids aren't bad or wrong for believing in the Boogey Man; they are just being kids. Neither are new franchisees bad or wrong for being in the Grind. They are just being new franchisees.

Someone once said a hero is an ordinary person who, under extreme circumstances, puts forth an extraordinary effort and produces outstanding results. Don't think that we are diminishing new franchisees by equating them with children. On the contrary, we equate them with heroes. They are up to creating something extraordinary with their lives and careers. This takes guts.

Skills

Throughout the Grind, franchisees are usually getting better at what they do. But because progress is slow, steady, and many times undetectable, they might lose sight of the progress they are making. It's kind of like watching grass grow or paint dry. It happens too slowly to see.

Skill development is what carries franchisees past the Grind and into Winning. Hopefully your franchisor is helping you identify areas to work on. If not, take it upon yourself to identify the skills you lack and create a plan to acquire them. Depending on the business and support level of the franchisor, an ideal scenario would be to budget several thousand dollars and at least one day a week to focus solely on skill development.

Does that sound excessive? Well, you can chop down a tree with a dull ax. It just takes a lot more swings, effort, and energy. Or you can stop chopping and invest time and money to sharpen the ax. Chopping becomes easier, your swing's more efficient, and you have energy left over to chop more trees. By developing your skills, you are sharpening your ax.

If this makes sense to you, this is because you aren't in the Grind. Logic and reality is suspended in the Grind and misperceptions rule. Many franchisees in the Grind think, "I can't afford to sharpen my ax right now. When the tree finally falls, I'll cut it up, sell the firewood, and then sharpen the blade." Others think, "If I stop swinging the tree will never fall. I can't take the time off to stop swinging." Some franchisees have spent such little time in skill development that they don't recognize there isn't any blade left at the end of their ax handle. "What's that thud?" they ask as the wood of the handle meets the wood of the tree. "I must not be swinging the ax handle hard enough!" *Thud. Thud. Thud. Thud.*

These are not stupid people. These are extraordinary people who have invested a lot of money for the right to create outstanding lives and careers. They simply forgot what it takes to learn and become masterful. It's been a long time since they had to build their knowledge and skills from scratch. Since many of the franchisor's staff has never owned a business, they can miss or fail to appreciate their franchisees' needs—and heroism.

Habits

In the Grind habits are beginning to gel. This is a critical time in the learning process, because as we said, "Practice doesn't make perfect, only perfect practice makes perfect. Practice makes permanent." Bad habits form as easily as good ones. Each business has high-priority activities that produce most of the results. Each business has minutia; those activities which suck a franchisee in, chew up time, and ultimately don't make a difference.

Forming winning habits will propel franchisees to a breakthrough in results and into the stage we call Winning. If the franchisee forms bad habits, they continue to "grind it out," feeling decreasing satisfaction and dramatically increasing their chance of failure. Most franchisees get into the flow of the business, find the right rhythm, and acquire the necessary KASH to experience Winning. But don't leave it to chance. Keep reading!

Strategies to Successfully Navigate the Grind

Work your business one day at a time. Plan your day and work your plan. Forget what happened yesterday. Deny yourself your right to worry about tomorrow. Today has enough worries of its own.

Chances are you have the necessary capital, desire, and energy required *today* to work toward creating your desired future. Focus today on developing the necessary KASH you need to succeed. Once today is complete, make a commitment to wake up tomorrow and do it again.

Get emotional support. Find someone in your life who instinctively knows how to pick you up when you're down. Call them for 10 to 15 minutes every morning to get you ready for the day. Let them be your emotional anchor. Tell them what you plan on achieving that day, and make it happen. Do it again tomorrow.

Acquire KASH.

Stay out of survival thinking. If you think you're failing, instead of playing to win, you are going to play not to lose. In baseball, when a pitcher is pitching not to lose, he starts aiming the ball and being too cautious. He becomes error prone and gets creamed. Eventually, his fear of losing manifests itself as losing. Make decisions you would make if you were playing to win.

> **Play to win. Do not play not to lose.**

Before you're in the Grind, think about the kind of decisions you would make if you were afraid of losing. What expenses would you cut? How would you modify your life or business? Write your answers down. That way, if you find yourself going down that tunnel, you can cut yourself off before you enter the darkness. Share your plan with your "emotional anchor" and perhaps with the franchisor so they can head you off.

Treat yourself gently. Mistakes are not bad or wrong, they just are. Learn and move on. You're supposed to be learning. If you aren't making mistakes, you aren't trying hard enough. If you're the type who, after making a mistake, likes to heap on guilt and blame, cut it out.

Be humble. Reach out for help. Let the franchisor contribute to you, helping you fix your problems fast. Find out how they see and define problems. Find out why they craft the solutions they craft. Get their vision. Stay in regular communication with those supporting you. The Grind comes from the disempowering belief that "There's no solution to my problem." You can't be working on a solution and be in the Grind at the same time.

Trust the learning process. Remember, you weren't born competent in your last position. No doctor ever removed anyone from their mother's womb, spanked their little butt, wrapped them in a blanket, and handed them to their mother proclaiming, "Congratulations, you just gave birth to an eight-pound, three-ounce vice president of human resources." No one gave your previous KASH formula to you. You earned it. You found a way to make it happen. The best predictor of future performance is always past results. If you found a way to make it happen in the past, chances are you'll find a way to make it happen now. You are resourceful. You can trust you. Don't forget it.

Work with the franchisor to get training to increase your knowledge and skills, consulting to quickly fix your problems, and coaching to hold you accountable for executing the knowledge you do possess and to help you manage your emotions.

How the Franchisor Can Help You Navigate the Grind

More Training

Have the support people watch you, monitoring your on-the-job performance. Have them focus on developing good habits, improving skills, and continuing to develop your knowledge base.

More Consulting

Don't be afraid to burn up the franchisor's phone lines. Keep close track of the key performance measures (labor cost, cost of sales, etc.) of your business. The franchisor will train you as to what they are and mean. Get these measures to the franchisor's support staff. Ask them what it means and get strategies to fix problems fast. If you disagree with the franchisor's solution, execute it anyway. Remember, your disagreement is coming from your past, and much of your past will be irrelevant in your new business model. Follow the franchisor's instructions closely until results prove otherwise.

More Coaching

Remember, your attitude is going in the toilet. You need consistent reminders of what your goals are and why you started your business in the first place. You need constant reminders that things will turn out fine over time. You need help moving through worry and you want the franchisor's support team to help you move through your stress in order to make better business decisions.

Winning

As franchisees acquire the necessary KASH to succeed, they begin to create positive outcomes. In the Grind, outcomes were something that happened to them; in Winning outcomes are something they've designed. Like a man pumping water, franchisees in the Grind spend tremendous amounts of time, money, and energy, pumping and pumping, disheartened by the mere trickle of water their pumping is creating. What they don't see is the pipeline full of water, which has yet to make it to the nozzle. Once the water starts flowing, it takes less and less energy to keep the water going. Less pumping produces more water. This is what Winning looks like. Winning isn't produced by a singular event; just like water doesn't flow by one mighty thrust of the pump. Winning is a process. You enter Winning through little victories, by learning to do the little things right, by steadily acquiring the KASH formula of success.

Winning creates a feeling of empowerment. Franchisees in the Grind feel trapped and powerless, like somehow *the business owns them.* In Winning, franchisees are empowered. They own their business. Keep in mind, all the time, *the business never changes.* The franchisees change! Their relationship to their business also changes. While in the Grind, owning businesses used to be something these franchisees did. Now it's who they are; they are entrepreneurs. They have made a successful personal transformation, like a caterpillar to a butterfly.

Now for the million dollar question: was it worth it?

Asking franchisees who are Winning this question is like asking a mother of a newborn baby if the labor pains were worth it. "Sure, it was worth it," the new mother smiles as she answers. She wouldn't have it any other way. The pain is a distant memory, replaced by the joy of being Mom.

Franchisees who are Winning will probably smile before they answer, too. "Yeah, it was worth it" they will most certainly respond. The pain of the Grind was replaced by the joy of being an entrepreneur.

Once the caterpillar becomes a butterfly, it's never again a caterpillar. It also seems that once employees become entrepreneurs, few will ever become employees again.

Keep in mind, there's nothing wrong with being an employee. Franchisees need and value employees. Without faithful and committed employees, most franchisees will never enter Winning. We are merely talking about personal transformation here. Getting franchisees to return to employee status is like getting a butterfly to return to being a caterpillar. Being an employee isn't wrong, the same way being a caterpillar isn't wrong. A butterfly is not better or worse than a caterpillar, just different. Entrepreneurs are not better or worse than employees, just different. The transformation process however, moves in one direction.

Franchisees in Winning see their desired future as occurring now. The freedom, challenge, flexibility, control, and other rewards they wanted when they started their business are now becoming reality. It's no longer a question of whether or not they will succeed, as they are Winning. It's now a question of how high they can fly.

Franchisees enter the Winning stage through a combination of their own personal effort and the franchisor's skill in imparting their KASH formula of success. Using a poker analogy, these franchisees are holding a Winning hand. However, they're not yet out of the woods; they can still fall back into the Grind. How? By folding the winning hand.

A franchisee of a vitamin retail chain once told a funny story about some of his customers. "When my new customers start taking our vitamin supplements, they feel ten times better. Some think, 'If I take ten times that original amount, then I should feel one hundred times better!' But instead of feeling better, they pollute themselves and feel ten times worse."

Why? They changed the Winning formula. They folded the Winning hand.

It can be the same with franchisees in the Winning stage. Many feel compelled to make "minor adjustments" like emphasizing certain aspects of their business and de-emphasizing others. Because they haven't completely grasped the KASH success formula, they may not fully realize the synergistic relationships and see the full impact of these decisions. They tamper with the Winning formula and in the process, fold their Winning hand. Then it's back to the Grind until they can figure out what went wrong.

When franchisees are in the Grind, a sophisticated franchisor focuses on training and consulting, imparting their knowledge and skills as fast as they can, making sure franchisees are focused on building Winning habits. They coach franchisees on maintaining a positive and healthy attitude. They encourage learning.

When franchisees enter Winning, a sophisticated franchisor will shift their support strategies to making sure franchisees *change nothing*, drumming the Winning formula into the franchisee's memory through sheer repetition. Franchisors should keep a watchful eye on these franchisees, but many franchisors don't understand this dynamic so they don't remain vigilant. They assume these franchisees will just keep doing what works and the world will be as it should be.

Because many franchisors don't understand this dynamic of human performance (the Winner's unwitting drive to fold the Winning hand), they aren't on the lookout for it. As you enter Winning, make sure someone is watching your back, documenting what you do, and holding you accountable for not changing anything!

Some franchisors offer competent ongoing coaching and support to their successful franchisees. Other franchisors spend most of their time and resources supporting franchisees in the Grind and less time with franchisees in Winning. If you're with the latter, consider hiring a professional business coach to make sure you don't change the Winning formula.

Franchisees in the Winning stage face a second risk. Although the business is growing, one person can only do so much. Steady growth will eventually cause an organizational breakdown unless franchisees develop their teams. The business needs to be more dependent on processes and systems and less dependent on entrepreneurs. The value entrepreneurs bring to the table must decrease and the value of what their teams bring must increase. God forbid if something unfortunate happens and the Winning franchisee becomes incapacitated. If the franchisee's team lacks the KASH to step up and continue in this franchisee's absence, the business may still fail.

Once it's clear the business will survive, it's imperative that franchisees impart the franchisor's KASH formula of success to their team. But franchisees who have successfully completed the Grind have difficulty letting go; they're afraid of going backward. Some hold on too tight, micromanaging, disempowering staff, and creating turnover. Others continue to work "medical residency" kind of hours and physically and emotionally burn out. Because they haven't fully developed their teams, some can't handle the growth and the business implodes. They become a casualty of Winning.

> **Franchisees in Winning should work with the franchisor to be trained as a trainer.**

Knowledge

Franchisees in the Launch are unconsciously incompetent. They don't know how incompetent they really are, so they're happy. Franchisees in the Grind are consciously incompetent. They know how bad they are and how far they need to go. Their joy turns to frustration. Franchisees in Winning are consciously competent. They know what they are good at and what they need to do to produce results. They are empowered with the experience of being able to make things happen. Their frustration turns to self-confidence. Yes, there are always additional things to learn, but they know enough to drive results. Their success depends more on how skillfully they execute their existing knowledge rather than learning new knowledge.

Attitude

Winning franchisees are empowered franchisees. They are re-engaged in the reasons they started their business in the first place. The future they desired when they started their business is now occurring. They have successfully navigated their learning curve and can see the finish line. All they need to do is to keep their foot on the gas, keep the wheel straight, and keep looking ahead.

Franchisees in the Grind drive their businesses by looking in their rear view mirror, fretting about costly mistakes in the past. Franchisees in Winning spend more time looking through the windshield, focused more on the road ahead. They only throw occasional glances in the rear view mirror as a reminder of where they've been.

Many franchisees in Winning start to develop genuine humility. The success formula of their business will shift again, this time becoming more dependent on the contributions of others and less dependent on the entrepreneur. Franchisees simply can't do it all, so they should stop trying. It's time for these "Superman" franchisees to retire their cape and red tights, put on their horn-rimmed glasses, and to return to Clark Kent status. Let Lois Lane and Jimmy Olsen shoulder some of the load.

Skills

Franchisees in Winning have developed and refined their personal skills. They are good at whatever they need to be good at to win. They have the ability to produce positive outcomes and handle whatever the business throws at them. Their next step is to become skillful trainers, developing the ability to successfully impart the KASH formula of the business to their employees.

Habits

Franchisees know the high-priority activities that produce the greatest results and spend their time engaged there. They have gotten into the rhythm and flow of the business. They are generating greater results with more ease and a high degree of predictability. One habit they probably need to drop at this point is self-reliance. It's time to include professional development and nurturing of staff into their day and groom themselves as a manager, transitioning from doing to delegating.

Strategies for Successfully Navigating from Winning to the Zone

Don't fold the Winning hand. Train and develop your staff, giving away the KASH success formula of the business, making sure everyone has the Winning hand. Refine your systems and document your processes and procedures. Let employees step up and contribute. Decrease your value so your employees may increase their value.

Get training from the franchisor on how to become a trainer and coach.

Request coaching from the franchisor, having them hold you accountable for staying the course and not folding your Winning hand.

An out-of-the-box strategy to drive performance is to volunteer to mentor another franchisee or to act as an assistant trainer in the franchisor's initial training program. Medical school professors have a saying called "See one, do one, teach one." They teach surgery by first letting the medical student observe (to build their knowledge), then do (to build their skills), and then teach (to build Winning habits). Just as a medical student won't teach what the medical student isn't already executing, you won't teach what you aren't executing. This is a brilliant way to permanently cement the Winning KASH formula in your memory.

How the Franchisor Can Help You

Less Training

You already know what it takes to win. Now it's about executing what you know. You do, however, want to be trained as a trainer so you can develop your staff. You also want to make sure you have a solid understanding of all the key performance indicators of your business and what they mean.

Less Consulting

You want to start developing a healthier sense of independence from the franchisor, building your skills so you can diagnose your own problems and have both you and your staff create your own solutions. The knowledge is now within you. Exercise it.

More Coaching

Work with the franchisor in goal setting and strategic planning. Request the operations support team to take on your goals as their goals. Since you are no longer concerned with simply surviving, it's time to re-engage in designing and realizing the future you originally desired for yourself and your family. Use the franchisor as your accountability structure, holding you responsible for executing your plan and realizing this future. Give them permission to challenge you and confront you when you are off track.

The Zone

When franchisees enter the Zone, they produce outstanding results as if they were on autopilot. They have fully committed the KASH success formula to memory. They are unconsciouly competent and brilliant execution has now become a habit. Keep in mind, most of what franchisees are looking to accomplish with their business will occur in Winning. Many Winning franchisees will not enter the Zone, nor is it a requirement for success. Peak-performing franchisees are far to the right of the franchisor's performance bell curve. These franchisees have highly developed teams and manage their businesses according to key performance measures. Rather than dismissing data and buying into the emotion of the Grind, they look past their emotion and take a healthy, daily objective look at results. They study the key performance measures, such as sales, labor costs, and product costs. They know what these numbers mean. If a number is off, they know where to look for the cause.

If labor cost is high, they will look into how they or their employees scheduled their labor. They will analyze customer counts during different periods of the day, looking for whether or not they were overstaffed and for changes in customers' shopping patterns. They will look for any fall-off in individual employees' sales productivity and see if the "dollars-per-customer transaction" is falling. Each measure will give them a separate plan of attack. They become an expert consultant to their own business and head off small problems before they become major ones. They play the Winning hand again and again, not feeling the need to fold it.

Just as golf's Tiger Woods doesn't need to think about the mechanics of his back swing before he tees off, the Zone franchisees no longer need to think about the mechanics of their businesses. Separating them from the KASH success formula of their business would require a lobotomy.

Picture yourself reviewing a detailed financial statement while sitting next to a CPA of a large public accounting firm. You and the CPA are looking at the same financial statement. You see lots of numbers that may not mean anything to you. The CPA sees patterns and a story behind the numbers. You may be looking at the same financial statement, but you aren't really looking at the same statement. Only one of you is looking through the eyes of a master.

So it is with peak-performing franchisees in the Zone. They don't see the business the same way as franchisees in the Launch, Grind, or Winning stages do. They have the characteristics of a master.

Transitioning from Winning into the Zone is not about doing more of what it takes to get into Winning. The difference is attitudinal. When in Winning, franchisees need to think about what they must do to win, create a plan, and then must execute the plan. Winning requires time invested in strategic thinking and planning. Franchisees in the Zone win automatically, with little thinking. They have so committed the KASH success formula to muscle memory, they now perform at masterful levels instinctively, with seemingly little thought or effort.

Knowledge

Peak-performing franchisees are walking encyclopedias, experts in their field. They know their customers, products, and where their industry is heading. They know the franchisor's corporate structure inside and out and where to go for support. They know what they need to know and stay on top of the changes.

Attitude

These franchisees are empowered with the sense of being able to design positive outcomes. They are Winners and they know it. Some become humble, attributing their success to the franchisor, their employees, and their Creator, instead of their own personal greatness. Others become puffed up; reveling in the "rock star" status the other franchisees give to them.

For some, their relationship to their business evolves again. No longer are they focused on just making money. They're now thinking about how to benefit others and the community. Their desire for success is replaced with a new desire for significance, profits for purpose. Others get caught up in the trappings of success, like bigger houses, fancier cars, expensive toys, and luxurious vacations.

Skills

Franchisees in the Zone expertly execute their knowledge. They have highly defined personal and organizational skill sets, being able to produce outstanding results with seemingly little effort.

Habits

The KASH model of success is fully committed to muscle memory. Peak performance is now a reflex, requiring little or no thinking. These franchisees know what activities produce the greatest results and structure their day to expertly execute these activities.

Peak-performing franchisees aren't without risk. Believe it or not, their greatest risk comes from Winning.

You may be asking yourself incredulously, "Winning???? How does Winning create risk?"

After conquering the last known civilization, famed military leader Alexander the Great cried out in anguish, "Alas, no worlds left to conquer." Alexander won. What was Alexander to do next?

Winning, like losing, means your game is over.

The thrill of living occurs in playing to win, not in the actual Winning. Winning is overrated. Playing to win is juicy.

Have you ever climbed a mountain? How long did you hang out at the top before you were bored out of your mind? Isn't it more thrilling to climb?

Peak-performing franchisees need to invent a new game to play or create a new mountain to climb, such as running multiple units, mentoring other franchisees, or getting more involved with their communities. If not, they will experience the anguish of having no more worlds left to conquer.

How the Franchisor Can Help You In the Zone

More Training

Not for you; but get training for your staff. Volunteer to help train other franchisees, giving you an experience of greater purpose. Allocate some time to mentor employees and at least one other franchisee who is mired in the Grind.

Less Consulting

Start relying on and challenging your staff to identify their own breakdowns and create their own solutions. Give them decision-making power. Use the franchisor's operational audits as their scorecard, an objective measure as to how your staff is doing.

More Coaching

Get agreement from the franchisor's support staff to never let you win. When it looks like Winning is inevitable, have them challenge you to design larger and loftier goals, goals so large you may never win or lose, designed simply to keep you motivated and in the game.

The Goodbye

When you contemplated buying your first home, did you think, "This is a house I will live in the rest of my life," or were you thinking shorter term? When you took your first job, did you think, "This is a good place to work for 40 years and then retire," or did you think it was a good place to cut your teeth, with thoughts of eventually moving on? For whatever reason, many people who look at franchises elect not to move forward because they can't find the business they want to operate for the rest of their lives. If they waited for the right job to come along that they wanted to work in for the rest of their lives, they would be unemployed. People who invest in franchises shouldn't look more than five to ten years out.

Many consultants will tell you the time to sell the business is when a business is at its peak market value. This doesn't always hold true in most franchises. That's like saying to a homeowner "The time to sell your house is at peak market value." From a financial perspective it's true, from a practical standpoint it's naïve. What if you have kids in high school? Do you pull them out and put them in a new school simply because your house has hit its peak market value? What if you simply enjoy your neighborhood and living in your town? Do you sever these relationships because the real estate market peaked? "Who cares about peak market value?" the homeowner thinks. "I like living here."

Just as there's a time to sell your home and change jobs, there will be an appropriate time to sell your business, and it may or may not be when it hits peak market value. There are other considerations. Before we discuss what those considerations are, let's first draw a boxing analogy.

Pretend you're the referee of a heavyweight championship fight. The champion is fighting a brilliant fight, landing combination after combination. The challenger is hurt, and appears dead on his feet. What do you do? You can wait for the champion to knock the challenger out cold and end the fight. Or you can end the fight by declaring the champion the winner by "technical knockout" or TKO as it's called. "The champion will eventually win," you think, "so why prolong the inevitable?"

The same is true with franchising. There are two times to sell, one is not necessarily better than the other. It's your business, so you get to choose which time is right for you.

1. When you have accomplished what you originally set out to accomplish and there's nothing left to accomplish. In other words, you won by a knockout. If you aren't inspired to train for your next fight, it's simply time to retire from fighting and choose your next sport.

2. When you know you will accomplish everything you're looking to accomplish, although it hasn't all been accomplished yet. It's just a matter of time, just around the corner. Sure, you could wait around for those results to occur, but work has lost its challenge and you don't feel like waiting. In other words, you declare yourself the winner by technical knockout. Again, if you aren't inspired to train for your next championship fight, it's time to retire from fighting and choose your next sport.

Sell your business when there are no worlds left to conquer; when you have nothing left to prove. Don't prolong the decision or you will have the same dissatisfying experience Alexander the Great had after the last civilization fell.

Remember, winning is boring; *playing to win is exciting*. Winning means your game is over. Winning, while certainly more rewarding than losing, is just as sad when you don't have the next game to look forward to. So play a new game! Don't wait for the sadness to come!

The Learning Curve of a Franchisee

Many franchisees hang around too long and become bitter. They long for "the good ol' days" when business was fun and they were inspired. They gossip with other franchisees and end up destroying the integrity of the franchisee/franchisor relationship. Because they have no worlds left to conquer, they simply hang around and take cheap shots at the franchisor and suppliers. Regardless of their age, they become like the crotchety old neighbor who sits on their rocking chair on the front porch, yelling at people who walk past. Not that the people walking past are doing anything wrong, but the crochety old neighbor is yelling because he or she has nothing better to do. The franchisor becomes a frequent and convenient target for franchisees who have nothing left to win and nothing better to do.

We're not asserting that these franchisees are necessarily doing anything wrong, the same way rocks aren't doing anything wrong when they hit the ground after being dropped. Rocks simply obey the laws of gravity. Franchisees are obeying the laws of behavior. To interfere with law of gravity, the rock has to be caught before it hits the ground. To interfere with the law of behavior, franchisees must either catch themselves or be caught by the franchisor before their attitude hits bottom. Because few franchisors understand the dynamics of normal human behavior, few look out for Winning or The Zone franchisees to fall. Asking franchisees to catch themselves is almost like asking the rock to catch itself.

Just as it's completely natural and expected for franchisees to generate positive attitudes in the Launch, it's just as natural for franchisees who win to become bitter if they don't create a new challenge. Again, this isn't good or bad, just the way it is. However, if they're not acting responsibly, they will react to their bitterness by creating problems between the other franchisees and the franchisor. And they won't have a problem finding an audience. The first people they will call are franchisees in the Grind!

Knowledge

Franchisees in the Goodbye stage of their business have expert knowledge. They have seen it all. While there will always be knowledge gaps to fill, new products being introduced, new vendors, new industry data, etc., these franchisees know what it takes to succeed and have committed the KASH success model to memory.

Attitude

There is a slow and steady erosion in their attitude. Many have accomplished what they originally were seeking to accomplish or what they were seeking to accomplish no longer motivates them. The business has lost its challenge and these franchisees are no longer inspired. Where work was once play, work is once again work. They start assigning the cause of their frustrations outside themselves. They think, "If my employees were more loyal, the franchisor was more responsive, my vendors weren't squeezing me, and my customers weren't so price sensitive, I would be happy." The business simply isn't fun any more. Since the business is working, there's little motivation to sell. However, their negative attitude will eventually impact their results, and the business will spiral downward.

Most franchisors report significant sales increases when such a business transfers ownership, often in double digits. What do these new franchisees have that the old franchisees don't? More knowledge? More skills? Better habits? Certainly not. They have a more productive attitude. Their attitude drives their results. New franchisees are inspired, old franchisees are tired.

Skills

These franchisees are highly skilled. However, one of their newly developed skills is cutting corners. Some become highly skilled gossipers and complainers. No longer motivated by achieving peak performance, they are more driven by not being hassled by employees, customers, and the franchisor. They become a "don't bug me," waiting to happen. They know how to cut back on the effort and still achieve some minimally acceptable performance. Over time, skills erode and negatively impact performance.

Others learn to delegate and start detaching more from the business. They develop other hobbies and interests which the business funds.

Habits

Many of these franchisees walk the path of least resistance. Chances are they have gotten out of the habit of personal development and continual improvement. They have gotten into the habit of cutting corners and just doing enough to continue to maintain their current lifestyle. As they are no longer focused on perfectly executing the high-priority activities which drive results, results will eventually flatten or spiral downward.

Franchisees in the Goodbye stage of their business usually say long goodbyes. They are like the last guests to leave the party, oblivious to the fact that the party is over. Because they have no other party to go to next, they just hang out.

These franchisees need coaching. They need the franchisor to sit down with them and revisit what they are looking to achieve. They need to be asked, "What's left to be accomplished? What more is there to do? What's next for you?"

But most franchisors don't measure attitude, just results. They don't measure whether or not franchisees are Winning (or have already won) *by the franchisee's definition of Winning.* Most don't know how to career coach franchisees out of their existing business and into an exciting new venture or challenge.

Overall, the franchising community has done an excellent job of developing themselves as trainers and consultants. Coaching is a largely ignored discipline within franchising, often confused with training and consulting.

These franchisees don't need to be trained. They already have the knowledge and skills they need to win. Nor do they need consulting; if they have an occasional operational problem they have the ability to fix it. They lack goals to inspire them. They haven't designed a future that they want to bring into the present. They are stuck. All the training and consulting in the world won't make a difference.

We recommend franchisees in Winning hire skilled business coaches to supplement the expert training and consulting many franchisors offer. Skilled coaches help these franchisees design, visualize, and construct the future, while letting the franchisor's operational support team help franchisees with the present.

When selling a business, there appear to be two types of franchisees' responses to the resale process. The first group may have sold businesses before or know others who have, and thus have a realistic idea of what their business is worth and what happens next. They sell a business the way others sell used automobiles. They know the business has a certain fair market value, and they research what it is. They calmly contact the franchisor's franchise sales representatives and alert them of their intentions. They also enlist the services of a business broker to generate leads. They exit with dignity and grace.

The second group dismisses the notion of "fair market value," assuming this concept doesn't pertain to their unique circumstances. They have no realistic idea what their business is worth. They assign a monetary value to their pain and suffering in the Grind and add that to the asking price of their business, like they are suing the new owners for damages. When the prospective buyers do their due diligence and question them about the business, they experience it as a personal attack. "More pain and suffering," they think. "I am going to have to raise the price of the business." They exit screaming and yelling, assuming someone screwed them.

How the Franchisor Can Help You with the Goodbye

More Training

Get training on how to value a business and what happens before, during, and after the resale.

More Consulting

Find out what businesses have sold for in the past. What's fair market value for your business? What terms should you consider? How will the franchisor support you and the buyer during the resale and transition of your business?

More Coaching

Selling a business is an emotionally taxing process. By this time you have so much mentally and emotionally invested in the business, separation is difficult. Additionally, what are you going to do next? Having nothing to do will make you want to hold on to the business longer, although you have somewhat lost interest. Work with the franchisor to help you design what's next, either inside or outside their franchise system.

Chapter Summary

Just as human beings evolve as they enter different stages in life, franchisees also evolve as they enter different stages in business. This evolution occurs through five distinct phases in linear order: the Launch, the Grind, Winning, the Zone, and the Goodbye. The franchisees' results and satisfaction level fluctuate from stage to stage. During each stage, franchisees are transformed by the KASH they acquire. Eventually, they experience the sense of control they were seeking when they started the business. Both work and life are good. They have internalized the KASH success formula of the business.

None of these stages are better or worse than any other stage, they simply are. Many franchisees however, resist the Grind and attempt to leapfrog right into Winning. Forcing the learning process seldom works; you get it when you get it. With an intelligent learning strategy, and close contact with the franchisor's trainers and operational support personnel, you will accelerate your learning curve and compress your timeframe from the Launch to Winning.

Chapter 7

The Evolution of the Franchisee-Franchisor Relationship

Back in Chapter 2, we looked at the different ways franchise candidates and franchisors answer the question, "What is a franchise?" You saw franchising in its lowest and simplest form as a distribution model, where franchisees sign a license granting them the right to distribute the franchisor's unique brand of products and services. Their relationship is defined by the language, intent, terms, and provisions of their agreement. This definition is impractically simplistic, assuming the relationship is static. And it doesn't take into account how both parties grow, communicate, and develop within this relationship.

More experienced and professional franchisors know this relationship is not defined by the language of any contract, much in the same way a marriage relationship isn't defined by the marriage certificate. The franchisee-franchisor relationship is a highly personal relationship. All the frailties, foibles, and imperfections of what it is to be a human being become visible in this particular type of relationship.

The Franchisee-Franchisor Relationship

There is love and respect. There is also anger and resentment. There are times of peace and times of war. Hang around franchisees and franchisors long enough and you will see their relationship break down, mend, break down, and mend again. There will be times of pushing and shoving, blaming and resenting, as well as peace and harmony, acknowledgment and gratitude. Their relationship runs the gamut from selfishness and pettiness and to selflessness and heroism, plus everything in between.

All the love, anger, and occasional dysfunction you'd witness when you attend a large family gathering also shows up in the franchisee-franchisor relationship at some point. This isn't bad, the same way large family gatherings aren't bad. It just needs to be anticipated and dealt with powerfully. In this chapter you will learn how.

Franchisees and franchisors who master this relationship become as one body, each acknowledging they need the other to win. Franchisees are relying on the franchisors to put together marketing strategies and operational processes and systems, which will help the franchisee generate cash flow to sustain operations. The franchisor is dependent on the royalty income the franchisees pay in. Both the franchisees and franchisors are completely reliant on the success of the franchisees' operations in order to survive, although they each come at it from different perspectives. Highly competent franchisees and franchisors put aside their petty differences, remembering they aren't each other's competition. The war they need to fight is for increased market share and franchisee profitability. Putting their personal differences into perspective, they recognize that neither party is going away. Then they find powerful ways to work with each other toward their common goals.

Again, this isn't bad, it's just the way it is.

World famous psychiatrist and Nazi concentration camp survivor Viktor Frankl once said, "An abnormal response to an abnormal situation is completely normal." Keep in mind 99 percent of the people who contact a franchisor to learn about their opportunity, don't move forward. While the 1 percent isn't abnormal, they aren't normal either. People don't "normally" take the actions necessary to define their lives and careers in their own terms. Franchisees are exceptional. Therefore their relationship with their franchisors also has the tendency of being exceptional; exceptionally good, exceptionally bad, and everything in between.

Greg Nathan, an internationally renowned franchise advisor, corporate psychologist, and founder of The Franchise Relationships Institute, has created a brilliant model which explains and identifies the normal shifting pattern of the franchisee-franchisor relationship. Nathan distinguishes a six-stage natural progression, which he calls the "Franchise E-Factor." Each stage is marked by the franchisee's and franchisor's distinct beliefs, emotions, actions, and levels of dependence and satisfaction with the relationship at that time. As the relationship matures, these beliefs, emotions, actions, and satisfaction levels also change. These stages in the franchise relationship are described in two of his books, *Profitable Partnerships* and *The Franchise E-Factor*. With his permission we provide in this chapter an outline of these stages and some tips for managing them. The six stages are:

1. Glee
2. Fee
3. Me
4. Free
5. See
6. We

The Glee Stage

The moment a potential franchisee makes the decision to join a particular franchise, they enter the Glee stage. They're filled with heightened emotions, ranging from joy to fear of the unknown, but underneath it all is a strong belief in the end they will be living the life they are designing for themselves and their families. They may not have even physically signed on the dotted line of their franchise agreement yet, but they have already mentally signed on. Having made a bold move to accept more responsibility for how their lives and career turn out, they feel empowered by the experience of having just altered their future.

The franchisee-franchisor relationship is marked by solid trust. The franchisee thinks, "Hasn't the franchisor done everything I asked them to? Haven't I been dealt with honestly and fairly throughout the investigation process? These are people I trust and respect, who believe I can get the job done and win."

Since most franchisees join franchise systems, which are a departure from what they are currently doing, their relationship is also marked by complete and total dependency on the franchisor's knowledge and experience. In the absence of any training and support from the franchisor, many franchisees will ultimately fail. Therefore, franchisees are vulnerable in the Glee stage. But they believe their franchisor will successfully impart the necessary KASH (knowledge, attitudes, skills, and habits) which will eventually liberate them. They have heart-to-heart discussions with the franchisor about their fears and concerns and have heard back, "We are always here for you," "You are our top priority," "We can't win if you don't win," and "If you have a problem, we are only a phone call away."

Tips for Managing the Glee Stage

Here are four tips for dealing with the Glee stage:

- Recognize it takes time to ramp up a business. Give yourself permission to learn. Most franchisees have produced in the past. Producers want to produce. However, early in the learning curve of the business, peak production is an unrealistic demand. Treat yourself gently.
- After you open, early on, you will understandably barrage the franchisor with questions about what to do from "My cash register receipt tape is jammed, and I don't know how to fix it" to "My employee didn't show up, now what do I do?" When contacting the franchisor with a question or concern, give them time to respond without creating a conflict. While your issues may appear urgent to you, most of what happens early on in a business is not life-threatening. At times, they will need 24 hours to get back to you. Treat others gently too.
- If you are lucky enough to have a strong grand opening, don't be put off if you see a lull after the event. Many times franchisees are successful in getting curious customers to try their products and services. These customers come in with a high frequency until the newness of your concept wears off and

their number of visits or calls will go down. Then they will shop you with lower frequency, but in a more predictable pattern. This downturn will be offset by your marketing efforts to solicit more customers.

- Accept that eventually the newness of your business will also wear off with you. This isn't bad, it's just the way it is as you get into the routines of the business. So be gleeful about being gleeful.

The Fee Stage

As you saw in the last chapter *The Learning Curve of a Franchisee*, franchisees enter a period called "the Grind," where it takes tremendous effort to generate marginal results because they are still learning what it takes to succeed in the business. Just as their relationship with their business goes negative for a period of time, so does their relationship with the franchisor.

Franchisees in Greg Nathan's Fee stage think, "My employees are getting paid, my vendors are getting paid, the franchisor is getting paid, but I'm not getting paid enough for my hard work! If the franchisor is my partner like they said, why do they want their money off the top? Forget what the franchise agreement says, they should make money when I make money! And what am I getting for this money? I have to do all the work!"

Franchisees in the Fee stage can become more demanding about the services they receive for their franchise fees. They look to cost justify the royalties they are paying in by demanding more.

As franchisees learn how to survive in business by spending their own money rather than their employer's money, they become more sensitive to where their money is going. Like any businessperson, they want to receive a return on their royalty investments. They raise their expectations of the franchisor, wanting such things as more services, higher quality, greater responsiveness, and more training for their staff. They also become more familiar with normal, everyday personalities and usual character flaws of the franchisor's employees and can become frustrated.

Just as in marriage, the Glee stage of the honeymoon is short-lived, replaced by the hard work of creating appropriate boundaries and setting realistic expectations of the marriage. In the Fee stage, the honeymoon period of the franchisee-franchisor relationship is also over, replaced by the "What have you done for me lately?" attitude of the franchisees.

Again, this isn't bad. It's just the natural process franchisees and franchisors go through as they work together to create an interdependent win-win relationship. They just aren't there yet.

Franchisees are still not fully competent in their business. So this stage is marked by a dependency on the franchisor, learning what they can count on the franchisor for, and what they need to count on themselves for.

Tips for Managing the Fee Stage

Here are three ways to negotiate the Fee stage:

- Consider that your royalty fees cover more than just whatever the franchisor has done for you lately. The franchisor has invested tens of thousands, hundreds of thousands, or perhaps even millions to develop the systems to get to where they are. Your royalty payments help the franchisor recapture past investments and provide for future investments to improve the system.

- Accept that employees of the franchisor are only human. Just as they weren't as perfect or superhuman as you may have made them out to be in the Glee stage, they're probably not as flawed or incompetent as you may make them out to be in the Fee stage.

- Continue to develop the business relationship *without fighting or taking things personally.* Allow time to manage your attitude before and after conversations with the franchisor's staff. Know what you want to take away from conversations and field visits before you have them. Develop a healthy sense of what you can and cannot count on the franchisor for and what you need to count on yourself for.

The Me Stage

Franchisees move into the Me stage when they finally get it, right down to their toes, that the franchisor isn't going to make them successful. Their success will be completely dependent on their ability to create results using the franchisor's business systems. Their mantra becomes "If it's to be, it's up to me!"

Franchisees enter the Me stage about the time they start generating results and gaining competency. Greg Nathan talks about a negative, self-serving "I did it all myself without help from anyone" kind of bias which can mark this stage. Franchisees may discount the value of the training and support they received as well as overlook the genius of the franchisor's systems and business model.

When things weren't going as well, it appeared as if it was the franchisor's fault. Now that results are happening, it looks like it's the franchisees' victory. "I'm succeeding *despite* the franchisor's incompetence," think some franchisees. From the franchisor's perspective, it seems it's a no-win situation.

Franchisees in the Me stage start Winning and experience a renewed sense of empowerment. Some will become rather egotistical, dismissing the franchisor's and other franchisees' contributions to their success. Others will become more assertive requesting, and sometimes demanding, the franchisor fund and implement initiatives they create. Franchisees can inject an "I know more than you do," attitude into the relationship, demeaning the franchisor's support staff and damaging the relationship.

In the Fee stage the franchisor falls off the pedestal franchisees had placed them on. In the Me stage the franchisor falls to the ground and franchisees jump up and down on the broken pieces.

In this stage franchisees assert their independence, a clear departure from their previous dependent relationship with the franchisor. Franchisees may exercise their independence by testing the boundaries of the franchisor's systems or even crossing them. Franchisors may respond to these challenges by using command-and-control techniques, like sending violation letters, demanding compliance, and correcting violations. Franchisees respond to these techniques by rebelling and pushing back even more. The relationship further breaks down.

Franchisees in this stage are similar to rebellious teenagers. In the teen years, parents appear stupid. From the teenager's perspective, it's a wonder the teenager has survived into the teen years with such incapable, incompetent parents. "I don't need my parent's advice," thinks the teen. "I know more than they do so I'm going to do what I want. They don't know what it is to be me."

Once again, the Me stage isn't bad. It's more of the natural progression toward creating a "oneness," an interdependent win-win relationship with the franchisor.

Tips for Managing the Me Stage

There are six things you can do to manage this stage:

- Give credit where credit is due. Recognize the efforts of the franchisors and franchisees before you who got the system and brand to where it is.
- Accept people as they are. The franchisor's staff was never as good as you made them out to be in the Glee stage and they're probably not as bad as you're making them out to be now.
- Honor your written and verbal agreements. Respect the boundaries of the operating systems and integrity of the brand. Don't cross a line you will come to regret later.
- Take time to be proud of your accomplishments, but don't sit on your laurels too long.
- You are starting to win. Don't change the Winning formula. Commit it to habit.
- Don't force your opinions down the franchisor's throat. Franchisors generally recognize the "million dollar ideas" come from the franchisees. Let your results speak for themselves and the franchisor and other franchisees will seek you out. You won't need a soapbox to stand on.

The Free Stage

As you can see, the relationship between the franchisee and franchisor has shifted from dependence to independence. As franchisees become more competent and independent, their relationship usually grows strained for a period of time. The Free stage is characterized by more franchisee competence, and thus more strained relations. Franchisees in the Free stage feel burdened by the meaningless and frustrating systems and control the corporation is putting on them. Put another way, as the franchisee grows more confident and competent in their business, they pick at and further test the boundaries of the franchisor's system. They may deviate from the norms and change the Winning formula of the business to their own detriment. The franchisor, once considered a trusted guide, may now be considered a storm trooper, who swoops down on them from their ivory tower, to lay siege to the franchisees' business for the sole purpose of telling them what to do.

Franchisees in Greg Nathan's Free stage, depending on their style, may get cynical and aggressive, battling with the franchisor's support team privately or publicly. Or they may fester and withdraw, choosing instead to gossip and create strained franchisee-franchisor relationships for other franchisees.

At the end of the movie *Braveheart*, Mel Gibson, portraying the captured Scottish rebel William Wallace, is strapped down to a table and offered the opportunity to either repent and die a quick death, or to maintain his rebellious attitude toward his rulers and die a slow, painful death. When asked for his decision, Gibson yells, "FREEEEEEEEEDOM!" And then the torturer does his business.

Some franchisees get stuck in this stage, and their relationship with the franchisor remains strained. Those who get stuck usually see one of three outcomes.

- They get frustrated with the franchisor and sell their franchise. *"FREEEEEEDOM!"*
- They frustrate the franchisor and the franchisor either forces a sale or terminates the franchisee's agreement for material breaches in their franchise agreement (if such breaches exist) or forces the franchisee into compliance. *"REPENT or die a slow tortured death!"*
- They learn to live together and stay out of each other's way, like two bad roommates sharing a college dorm room.

Franchisees who successfully navigate through the Free stage unpredictably, almost miraculously, experience an epiphany, a big "ah hah!" which dramatically alters the future of their franchisee-franchisor relationship.

Tips for Managing the Free Stage

Here are four ideas for dealing with the Free stage:

- Remember your commitments and honor your franchise agreement. No doubt at some time during your investigation of the franchisor, you agreed to conform with and master the franchisor's business system. You made a promise so keep it and stop resisting. The franchisor is on your side, (you just think they aren't). The franchisor is not trying to control you (you just think they are). Franchisors must protect both their investment and other franchisees' investments. Don't back them into a corner. Stay in problem-solving mode and away from fighting. Remember the value of this relationship because it's what you paid for.

- Don't let open and unaddressed issues fester. Get closure. If you need to bring a third party in to be heard, do so. Don't fight. Bring in a third party who will support you and help you stay in problem-solving mode.

- Don't gossip and don't listen to gossip. Gossip is often defined as bringing your problems to someone who has no authority to resolve your issues. Gossip plants the seeds of ill will and destroys companies. Don't participate.

- Create win-win solutions. You know enough about both your business and the franchisor's business to recommend solutions where you both win. Get in their world. Franchisors are primarily concerned with four things: recruiting more franchisees, collecting more royalties, maintaining franchisee-franchisor relations, and building the brand. Show them how they can implement your suggestions to drive royalty collections creating results in one or more of these four areas. If they see your suggestions as all cost and no benefit, of course they will resist implementing them.

The See Stage

The franchisee gets it. They were blind to it, but now they get it. They see if every franchisee within the franchisor's system pushed, pulled, fought with, and demanded things of the franchisor the way they do, the franchisor would die. And, most everyone would lose their investment. The franchisee sees the systemwide impact of their behavior and negative relationship. They see if they re-channeled their energy into creating positive relations with the franchisor and driving their own business, rather than in fighting, resisting, or gossiping, everyone is better off. They understand that the franchisor isn't going anywhere. They realize that their negative relationship with the franchisor can either be a short-term problem or a long-term one and they get to say which.

They see they are part of a larger organic system, a bigger body consisting of the employees and owners of the franchisor, the franchisees, and the franchisees' suppliers. All are committed in their own way to build the brand and always were. As famed cartoonist Walt Kelly's creation Pogo once said, "We have met the enemy and he is us!" The franchisee sees over time they slowly forgot how connected they were and still are. There's recognition that the franchisor doesn't measure success the way the franchisee measures success. The relationship is no longer about one party winning and the other losing. The franchisee gets it. *Both parties need to win!* This invites mature, intelligent, commercially minded strategizing and problem-solving, not petty, immature fighting, bickering, and gossiping.

The connectedness they experienced during the Glee stage starts to come back.

The relationship immediately begins to mature from an independent relationship to an *interdependent relationship*, which is all the franchisee and the franchisor wanted in the first place.

Tips for Managing the See Stage

Here's what you can do in the See stage:

- Mend fences with the franchisor's support staff. In the past, you probably tweaked some noses, caused some problems, and bruised some egos. 'Fess up. Take responsibility for your actions and take the initiative to repair relationships that need repairing. Just because you are ready to forgive and start over, don't assume others are. It takes two parties ready to move on in order to get to the next stage.
- Mend fences with existing franchisees. Chances are you

enrolled others in your battles and gossiped with them about the franchisor. Perhaps you've trained other franchisees to relate to you as a troublemaker or are, at least, partly responsible for other franchisees being mired in their Free stage. 'Fess up again. Invite franchisees to follow you into your new, mature See stage.

- Get involved. The franchise is one body with many members. Consider becoming an active, productive member of the larger body. In the past, perhaps you were a hemorrhoid, occasionally flaring up, gaining some attention, and causing general irritation until someone gave you what you needed to go away. You could now become the belly button, serving no real purpose, passively coming along for the ride, and occasionally gathering lint. Or you can become the eyes, ears, hands, and feet of the organization, gathering data, testing new initiatives, and paying attention to the big picture for the benefit of all. You get to say which.

The We Stage

The See stage opens the door to broader possibilities available only in the We stage. The door was always there, you just needed to look beyond your independent thinking to see it. This stage is characterized by mature, objective, global, problem-solving, strategic, interdependent thinking. The franchisor is no longer the enemy. The battle is for market share, not about who is right or wrong. The relationship is fully mended, assuming of course, the franchisor is fully with the franchisee in the We stage. *Less competent franchisors also get stuck in the Me stage*, thinking the "ungrateful" franchisees are there to serve them. "It's my company," they think. "If they don't like it, they can get out!"

Greg Nathan suggests that to create a franchise culture of We, a few things have to happen.

1. Mature franchisees have to be Winning, getting both an acceptable return on their investment and living the lifestyle they desired when they first joined the franchise system.
   The franchisor must also be on a Winning track.

2. Both the franchisees and franchisors must understand the other's viewpoint and respect it as if it was their own.

3. Both the franchisees and franchisors must understand and respect each other's style and decision-making processes.

4. The franchisees and the franchisor must each be fully committed to the other's success. The franchisor must think, "When a franchisee fails, I fail." And franchisees must come from, "If my franchisor isn't Winning, I'm not Winning."

Tips for Staying in We

There are three tips for the We stage:

- Be an active and positive participant in networking with others in your system. Be a "We" advocate and evangelist. Most successful franchisees experience an obligation to give back to the whole. In the process you will experience a greater sense of purpose, and with it, results.

- Sit on committees or assist with mentoring new franchisees. You know what it takes to win and you experienced the four stages of the learning curve of a franchisee and the six stages of the franchisee-franchisor relationship. You can help others navigate their stages.

- Chances are by now you have become a thought leader in your chain. Use your influence and leadership for the benefit of the greater body.

From Glee to We

In the Figure 7-1 from Greg Nathan's *Franchise E-Factor* you will note a natural progression from dependence, to independence, to eventual interdependence. Franchisors who have successfully created interdependent relationships with franchisees have a high probability of creating a lasting brand with significant value.

Franchises that are mired down in the Me or Free stages stand a high probability of imploding from infighting, with many people getting caught in the crossfire. A famous teacher once said, "A house divided amongst itself cannot stand." When franchisors and franchisees forget they are on the same team, the unified brand disintegrates into a divided house. When conflicts arise, franchisees and

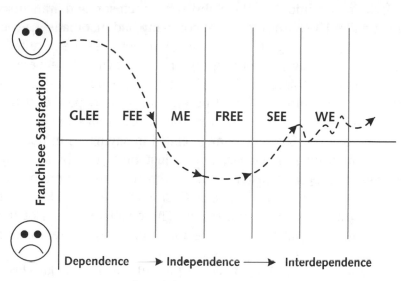

The Franchise E Factor was developed and
copyrighted by Greg Nathan

Figure 7-1. The Franchise E Factor®

franchisors invest time, energy, and money on guaranteed lose-lose outcomes, which tarnish the brand, destroy the value of their investments, and severely damage the franchisee-franchisor relationship.

That isn't to say the franchisee-franchisor relationship isn't supposed to have its peaks and valleys. Like any relationship, it does. But if the franchisee-franchisor relationship is currently in a valley, as long as it was built initially on a foundation of trust, respect, and commitment, the relationship will see a peak again.

If not, the franchisee-franchisor relationship has a tendency to keep spiraling downward. In these instances, there may be a point where the relationship is so damaged, the parties have so much emotionally and financially invested in their opposing opinions, that civil war breaks out. Nobody wins.

When you are investigating franchisors, pay particular attention to where franchisors and franchisees are in this relationship scale. If the franchisees and franchisor are at odds, don't immediately dismiss the opportunity. Dig deeper. As long as there is mutual trust and both parties continue to listen, they may just be in the valley leading to the next peak.

Back in the mid-80s, the Subway® franchisor and franchisees were at odds. The Subway® parent company had just made a sweeping decision, requiring all new Subway® franchisees are required to bake fresh bread every morning rather than having it delivered by bread suppliers. "More work!" cried out some franchisees. "Why break what isn't broken?" cried others. For a short period of time, their relationship soured. However, the decision was the right one and sales took off. Some customers called in saying, "I'm not interested in ordering sandwiches, may I just buy your bread?" New stores also ramped up faster. Subway® created a dynamic point of difference from other food chains. Customers became excited and new customers flocked to the stores. The delicious aroma of fresh baked bread hung in the air while they anxiously waited to order their food.

Consider where Subway® would be without fresh baked bread. Initially, not everyone was happy with this decision.

Success cures many ills.

Note: For more details on the Franchise E-Factor we would recommended *The Franchise E-Factor* and *Profitable Partnerships,* both by Greg Nathan and published by The Franchise Relationships Institute. Available from www.franchiserelationships.com.

Part Two

Investigating Franchises

Chapter 8

Locating Franchise Opportunities

By completing Part One of this book, you now have a thorough understanding of what franchising is and isn't and what it takes to win. If we haven't succeeded in scaring you off, it's time for you to explore the different options available to you.

Franchising experts estimate there are currently over 2,000 franchise opportunities in the United States, representing more than 70 different industries. Additionally, it's estimated that anywhere from 200 to 250 new companies start franchising each year. With so many different franchise options available, you can once again ask yourself the question, "What do I want to be when I grow up?" If you like what you already do for a living, but it's just time to start doing it for yourself, you may find a franchise in a similar field or industry to the company you will be leaving.

If what you do no longer excites you, consider doing a career "extreme makeover" by looking at franchises completely unrelated to your current career.

Whether you are looking to do something materially similar or radically different, be like a kid in a candy store and enjoy the shopping experience.

For people beginning to explore franchising, franchise opportunity web portals are the first place most people look. There are many franchise-specific web sites from which to choose. Many franchisors advertise on more than one of these web sites, so don't be surprised if you see the same franchise opportunities popping up again and again. Visit multiple sites. Each has its own little twist, like articles and educational information, newsletters, search capabilities, or other unique features. The sites we recommend you explore (in no particular order) are:

Franchise Opportunity Web Sites

- www.entrepreneur.com
- www.franchise.org (The International Franchise Association web site)
- www.franchiseopportunities.com
- www.franchisesolutions.com
- www.franchisegator.com
- www.franchiseforsale.com
- www.franchise.com
- www.bison.com
- www.franchiseworks.com
- www.franchiseemporium.com

Franchisors advertising on these sites post one- or two-page online brochures, giving brief descriptions of their history, their product or service, what makes them unique, who their target customer is, who their target franchisee is, and what their total investment is. While few of these web sites offer links to the franchisor's home pages, you can easily find the home pages by typing the franchisor's name into an Internet search engine.

Depending on the franchise opportunity web site you visit, you should find anywhere from 200 to 400 or more franchise opportunities to comb through.

If you want to request more information about a particular franchise opportunity or speak to a franchisor representative, all you have to do is fill in your contact information on the franchisor's contact form. Each franchise opportunity web site follows the same process.

Franchise Brokers

Because there are so many different franchise opportunities available and people looking into franchising are so time-starved, an interesting branch of business brokers have emerged known as "franchise brokers," "franchise referral agents," or "franchise coaches."

Franchise brokers are usually experienced business people who specialize in working with people looking to start franchises. Most franchise brokers will know what franchises are available in particular markets along with the skills, aptitudes, and capitalization a franchise candidate needs to succeed. Like any normal bell curve distribution, the value that franchise brokers offer varies from broker to broker. Some offer their clients expert professional guidance and outstanding one-on-one career coaching. Others simply shove a few franchise brochures in their clients' hands and say "Call me if you're interested."

Most franchise brokers offer their services to their clients free of charge. If a client joins a particular franchisor the broker recommends, their commissions are paid for by the benefiting franchisor. Because you benefit from the experience of working with a strong professional franchise broker without incurring high upfront fees, we recommend you take advantage of their services.

Keep in mind, franchise brokers only work with a smaller selection of the many different franchise opportunities that exist. Since franchise brokers have a large inventory of franchisors who work with them, and their clients are free to investigate any franchise they wish to on their own, their clients seldom feel limited.

There are several hundred brokers across the United States and abroad, so you will likely find a broker who lives in or knows your area.

There are four major companies who have the most experience. They are (in no particular order):

- Franchoice (www.franchoice.com)

- The Entrepreneur's Source (www.theEsource.com)
- Frannet (www.frannet.com)
- Franchise Buyer (www.franchisebuyer.com)

Magazines

Entrepreneur Magazine is the gold standard publication for people looking to start businesses. They often run articles that highlight franchising. The January issue (often called "The Franchise 500 Issue") rates the top 500 franchisors according to a proprietary rating scale.

Franchise Expos

The International Franchise Association holds annual franchise expos (called the International Franchise Expos or IFE), usually one on the East Coast and another on the West Coast. These expos give you the opportunity to check out many different franchise options and ask questions of franchisor representatives. You can go to www.franchise.org and check their events page for details.

Newspapers

The *Wall Street Journal* and *USA Today* both regularly highlight the franchise industry. *USA Today* runs a special franchise feature every Wednesday and the *Wall Street Journal* does the same every Thursday.

After you have identified one or more franchisors that you want to investigate, proceed to the next chapter. You will learn how to conduct a thorough, step-by-step franchise investigation to determine whether or not you fit a particular franchisor's profile of a successful franchisee. You'll also learn if the franchise opportunity you're investigating can produce your desired results with a high degree of probability.

Chapter 9

Following a Six-Step Franchise Investigation Process

As you read this book you may be struck by an unusual paradox, which affects franchising. The more entrepreneurial and comfortable with risk a person is, the less likely they are to follow systems that others create. The people most likely to invest in a franchise are also the most likely to resist following the system they just bought into. While this is certainly not true in all cases, it's been observed in most situations.

Many high-risk takers resist following systems, yet they are generally strong producers who generate consistently great results. If you read through the history of their performance reviews you'd see a consistent pattern of supervisor feedback which reads like, "Steps on people's toes and routinely ignores internal rules and regulations. However, she (or he) produces great results. Pain in the neck, but I wish I had ten people like her (or him)."

Does this sound like you?

If so, as you investigate different franchises, know this resistance-to-systems dynamic exists. Understand that the stronger your resistance, the more you increase your financial risk. Even in the face of resisting systems, if you still found a way to produce consistently great results in the past, chances are you'll probably also produce great results in franchising.

The best predictor of future results is past results.

If you have produced for others, chances are you will continue producing for yourself. Your past job and career didn't make you successful. You did the work necessary to win. Your company may have offered you the potential to win, but you brought winning into actuality. Winning isn't what you do, winner is who you are.

If you've produced consistently poor results in the past, chances are you will produce consistently poor results in the future. Being in business for yourself is probably not going to change this dynamic.

Remember, regardless of the franchise you investigate, every franchise has its own distinct KASH (Knowledge, Attitude, Skills, Habits) formula for success. You have your own personal KASH formula for success. The goal of your investigation process is to find a franchisor whose KASH success model closely matches your personal KASH model.

Keep in mind, you probably won't find a perfect match, nor do you need to. You want to find a close match. The first several chapters of this book were designed to make you look inward, to help you determine your personal KASH model for success. Let's call this your "starting KASH." Your franchise investigation process will answer the following questions.

1. What are my goals? (from Chapter 5)
2. What is my "starting KASH"? (from Chapter 6)
3. What is the franchisor's KASH formula for success?
4. What KASH am I currently missing from this formula?
5. What training and support is the franchisor making available to fill in my KASH gaps?
6. What is the franchisor's track record for helping franchisees like me acquire the necessary KASH to win?
7. What is the probability I will achieve my goals with the franchisor's business model?

Regardless of how sexy the business appears, how cool the products or services are, how enjoyable the customers seem, or how well you think you fit in, if the franchise opportunity will not deliver your desired results with a high degree of probability, *it's the wrong franchise for you.*

The easiest way to compare different franchise opportunities is to create a simple visual display that you can update as you gather information. We offer you a sample display later in this chapter.

In this chapter you will learn how to research and compare opportunities against their ability to deliver your "must have" and "wish to have" goals from Chapter 5. You may be a person who researches only one business at a time. Or you may be a person who compares two or more franchises at a time. Either way, the criteria you will use to compare and contrast businesses, regardless of whether or not they are in the same industry, is their ability to deliver your desired lifestyle.

Aside from evaluating the franchise as a viable business opportunity, *it's equally important to evaluate the franchisor as a viable franchisor.* Remember, a franchisor needs to be brilliant in four key areas.

1. **Marketing.** The franchisor has to know how to build a brand that means something to the consumer. The franchisor must have systems in place, which if followed, are proven to help you establish the same brand equity in your local market.

2. **Recruiting high-quality franchisees.** The success of a franchisor is built on a foundation of successful franchisees. Skilled franchisors know how to identify and recruit franchisees that will succeed in their system and say "no" to everyone else.

3. **Training and developing franchisees into peak performers.** Peak-performing franchisors know what it takes to win and have their KASH model well identified. They know how to transfer their knowledge and develop their franchisees' skills. They help franchisees acquire the "mindset of a master" and hold franchisees accountable for consistently executing the high-priority activities that produce most of the results. They track franchisees' progress and offer consistent and valuable feedback on how to get to the next level. They value and embrace continual learning. Learning and advancement are strong fibers woven into the fabric of the organization's culture.

4. **Creating positive franchisee and franchisor relationships.** Excellent franchisors have created a powerful, interdependent relationship with their franchisees. They work together to increase brand equity rather than fight to either control or resist being controlled by the other party.

To build a strong national brand, a franchisor must have a business opportunity that consistently produces great results and, at the same time, be a brilliant franchisor. When a franchisor is missing one or the other, this is a franchisor's recipe for future problems.

In this chapter we are going to offer you a simple, six-step process for investigating a franchise. By following this process, you will complete both an investigation of the franchise and a rigorous self-examination as to whether or not you fit into a particular franchise system.

Although we will teach you the process, understand that outstanding franchisors have their own franchisee investigation processes, which may or may not mirror this one. If this is the case, defer to and follow the franchisor's investigation process, adopting the tools we will offer you in our process. If they don't have a step-by-step investigation process, consider taking the franchisor through this process. Also keep in mind, any franchisor who doesn't have a clearly defined franchisee investigation process, *probably also doesn't have a clearly defined business model.* Beware of these franchises!

In the previous chapter you learned where to go to explore different franchise opportunities. Once you have narrowed your options to the two or three franchises you wish to explore, use this systematic approach to reduce your choices to your best single fit.

Overview of the Six-Step Franchise Investigation Process

The six steps are as follows:

- Step One: Initial Interview
- Step Two: Qualification
- Step Three: Reviewing the UFOC and Franchise Agreements
- Step Four: Franchisee Validation, Data Gathering, and Analysis

- Step Five: Visiting the Franchisor's Home Office
- Step Six: The Yes/No Decision

Step One: The Initial Interview

The first step is an initial interview and presentation of the franchise concept, usually conducted by telephone or in person with a franchise sales representative. This interview is a 45- to 90-minute give-and-take of information. This is a "getting to know each other" step, where you help the franchise sales representative understand who you are, what makes you successful, and what you're looking to accomplish. The franchise sales representative, in turn, helps you understand who the franchisor is, what makes the franchise opportunity unique, and who makes a successful franchisee. You both begin the process of determining whether or not your skills and aptitudes match the skills and aptitudes required to succeed within the franchise. It's designed to give you a quick gut read as to whether or not the franchisor's KASH model of success is in alignment with your personal KASH model and if your objectives can be met with a high degree of probability.

Step Two: Qualification

Qualification is either conducted by telephone or sometimes in person, depending on whether or not the franchisor you're investigating has a local franchise sales representative who can meet with you. The purpose of step one was to give the franchisor a quick sketch of who you are, what your objectives and goals are, as well as giving you a general understanding of the franchisor and the business model. The purpose of step two is to gather and offer more specific details. The overall objective of step two is to determine whether or not there is a fit *from the franchisor's perspective*. If you create an open and honest dialogue with the franchisor, *they will probably see the potential fit before you do* because they have an insider's perspective on what it takes to win. If, for whatever reason you don't possess the necessary KASH or capital (from the franchisor's perspective), you want to find out now before you have invested any significant time and money into the investigation process. If, from the franchisor's perspective, you do have the proper capital and KASH, you will still need to verify the details and performance levels of the other franchisees to see whether or not there is a fit from your perspective.

Step Three: Reviewing the UFOC and Franchise Agreements

During step three, you will conduct a *business* review of the terms and conditions of the Uniform Franchise Offering Circular (UFOC) and make sure you and the franchisor are in material agreement on all major points. The UFOC is a document the Federal Trade Commission mandates each franchisor to offer franchise candidates. Some states may require more disclosure information in the UFOC than the FTC does.

There are two ways to look at a UFOC. The first way is through the eyes of a businessperson. From a business perspective, does the Offering Circular make sense? Can you live with the terms and commitments of the agreement? Later, you can bring the UFOC to an attorney who will review it from a legal perspective. At this stage you may not feel the need to bring in legal counsel since you're still gathering data. Once you've established the fit, there will be time to conduct a legal review. At this stage, conducting a legal review may be premature and an unnecessary expense. However, it's time to become aware of what the business commitments look like and whether or not you're willing to honor them. If, for whatever reason there are commitments or obligations in the franchise agreement you cannot live with, you will end the process here. If you can honor these commitments with integrity, you proceed to the next step.

Step Four: Franchisee Validation, Data Gathering, and Analysis

The purpose of step four is to interview franchisees, gather data, compare the information you receive from franchisees with what you received from the franchisor, and determine whether or not you'll produce your desired results with a high degree of probability. This is a period of intense data gathering and heavy analysis. Here's where you test the veracity of the franchisor's systems and determine whether or not the franchisor is a skilled one. If the franchise appears to produce your desired lifestyle with a high degree of probability, it's time to make some investments in professional advice. You'll need to have a franchise attorney review your UFOC and an accountant review your business plan.

Step Five: Visiting the Franchisor's Home Office

Never do business with people you haven't met. Franchising at its best is a highly personal relationship. You are entrusting your dreams and capital into the care of the franchisor's leadership. Decisions made on the executive level impact whether or not you are positioned to hit your personal objectives. Go to their corporate offices, meet the decison makers, shake their hands, look them dead in the eye, and ask tough questions. You've already evaluated the business model against its ability to produce your desired results. Now it's time to evaluate the competency level of the franchisor as a franchisor.

Step Six: The Yes/No Decision

Now it's time to make up your mind about whether you design a new life and career of your choosing or to go back to the way it was.

Now that you know the process in general, let's look at the steps individually.

Step One: The Initial Interview

What does a successful initial inteview look like? At the end of the 45- to 90-minute conversation, this is what should have occurred.

1. You offered the franchisor a basic understanding of your background, skills, aptitudes, and financial resources in order to determine, from the franchisor's perspective, whether or not you fit the profile of a successful franchisee.
2. You clearly stated and the franchisor clearly understands both your financial and "quality of life" goals. You received the franchisor's commitment to tell you if they feel your goals cannot be achieved with a high degree of probability.
3. The franchisor clearly communicated to you the most important details about their business model in order to help you determine how your objectives can be met utilizing their skills, systems, and training.

4. You and the franchisor are both clear as to what the next action steps are and you have both agreed to take these steps.

The first indicator of whether or not you are dealing with a skilled franchisor is how they conduct this initial conversation. They should know the questions they need to ask to begin qualifying you as a prospective franchisee. They should also know the type of information you will be looking for to qualify them. They should be prepared with both.

Prior to this meeting or telephone conversation, some franchisors will ask that you fill out a simple online questionnaire. If this is the case, skilled franchisors will prepare for this meeting by reading these questionnaires ahead of time. If you get a sense the franchise sales representative isn't prepared for your conversation, raise a red flag. Again, if they don't have a well thought-out, well organized, and well executed franchisee recruitment process, it's reasonable to assume they don't have a well thought-out, well organized, and well executed franchise business model either.

Part of being a skilled franchisor is to be a skilled franchisee recruiter. Being a skilled recruiter demands *being a skilled interviewer*. If a franchisor doesn't ask pertinent questions about your ability to succeed within their franchise system, this is a cause for concern.

When asked questions, answer openly and honestly. Begin to work in partnership with the recruiter to evaluate whether or not there is a match. Good franchisors won't try to hard sell you. They merely present their opportunity and let their results stand on their own merits. Good franchisors will be as concerned with the quality of the match as you are. Go into the meeting trusting this, unless you discover a reason not to.

Questions you should expect to be asked include ones about:

Your Career
- What is your work history?
- What do you currently do?
- What are your responsibilities?
- Why are you looking to start a business?
- What are you looking for a business to produce?
- What would you like to be earning in one, three, and five years?

- What is your education?
- How does what you wish to be earning compare to your current earnings history?
- How much cash each month does it take to run your household?
- What other financial objectives do you have? (such as an increase in net worth, etc.)
- What does winning look like to you?

Your Family

- Are you married? If yes, does your spouse support you starting a business?
- Do you have children? How many, what ages?

While some of these questions may be illegal or inappropriate to ask if you were applying for a job, this isn't the case with franchising. Starting a franchise will impact your personal relationships. Franchisors will want to know if you have communicated your intentions to others who will be impacted and whether or not you have their support. Franchisors don't face the same restrictions as employers as to what they can and cannot ask you during an interview. Highly skilled franchisors will ask you highly personal questions.

Your Other Career or Franchise Options

- What other concepts have you looked at?
- What kept you from moving forward with these concepts?
- What other career options have you investigated? Why?

Franchise recruiters will want to know what stopped you from moving forward in the past. Predictably the same issues may keep you from moving forward in the present. They know that roughly 1 percent of the people who inquire about a franchise move forward. They want to know why you were among the 99 percent who didn't move forward when investigating other franchise systems and what makes you think you will be among the 1 percent who will be going forward with them. They will want to know who they are competing with. It's in your best interest to let them know who else you are looking at as it may help your negotiating position later.

Your Personal Finances

The franchise recruiter may ask you questions such as:

- If I were to review your financial statement, what is the amount of cash you have available to invest?
- Leaving out personal items such as furniture and cars, what would you ballpark your net worth to be?
- If I were to pull your credit report, what would it say?

Although it may feel uncomfortable to discuss personal finances with someone you don't know, it's in your best interest to do so. A skilled franchisor is going to ask you these questions upfront so they know whether or not you have the necessary capital or the ability to raise it. The number one reason for business failure is undercapitalization. If you are open and honest with the franchisor, you'll know whether or not you are undercapitalized in the first conversation. Not only do you need the necessary KASH (knowledge, attitude, skills, and habits) you also need the necessary cash.

After you've answered the above questions, the franchisor should offer you a good overview of its franchise model. Although neither of you will be able to tell with a high degree of certainty whether or not the franchise is a match for you, you should be able to tell whether or not you're a potential fit. If, after listening to and evaluating the information a franchisor provides, you get a sense you aren't a good fit, end the process and begin investigating other franchises.

A franchisor should be able to offer you information or answer your questions about the following:

1. The mission of the franchisor
2. The history of the franchisor: How did this franchise get started?
3. The number of units open and under development
   - What markets are being targeted for development?
   - What are the development plans in your area?
   - Long-term growth objectives: How many units does the company eventually want and over what timeframe?
   - Have any units failed? If so, how many, and why?

4. What is their concept?
   - What is their product or service?
   - What makes it unique?

- What need does it fill in the marketplace?
- How is it priced?
- How many employees does it require?
- How is it promoted?
- Who is the competition?
- How does the franchisor differentiate its products or service from what its competitors offer?

5. What is the industry?
   - Size and data
   - Why is this industry attractive?
   - What does the future of the industry look like?

6. Who is the customer?
   - Demographics
   - Buying behavior
   - Why should they do business with your franchise?

7. How do you find customers?
   - Advertising strategies, marketing strategies, PR strategies, etc.

8. Where is the concept located?
   - What type of location is needed?
     - Mall, strip center, office park
     - Do I rent or buy?
     - Do I remodel or build?
     - How much space do I need?

9. What is the profile of a successful franchisee? What are the traits, characteristics, experience, strengths, background, education level, aptitudes, liquidity, and net worth of a successful franchisee?

10. What are the investment options?
    - Single unit, multi-unit, etc.
    - What is the investment level?
      - How much cash is needed?
      - How much can be financed?
      - Where do I get financing?

11. What kind of support do franchisees receive?
   - Location support
   - Assistance with financing
   - Assistance with construction
   - Initial and ongoing training
   - Marketing, graphic design, and advertising promotional support
   - Ongoing business coaching
   - Product research and development

You should be able to offer and gather this information in 90 minutes or less.

Cut to the Chase: How Much Money Can I Make?

Most likely, earnings information won't be made available to you in the first conversation. Franchising is regulated by the Federal Trade Commission, which has a process and structure for franchisors to follow in providing you with this information. Since there is legal risk to providing earnings information, most franchisors elect not to. If a franchisor tells you, "It's illegal for me to give you this information," realize this is an inaccurate statement. The truth is, any franchisor can legally give you this information; they just have to present it in accordance with FTC guidelines. As a matter of fact, a recent study commissioned by the International Franchise Association Foundation showed about 25 percent of franchisors do provide some form of earnings information in their UFOC. Franchisors who don't offer earnings statements to prospective franchisees don't do so for the following three reasons:

1. Historical franchisee or corporate unit financial performance do not make a compelling case for you to move forward, (this could be because of poor performance or because they are a young franchise with a lot of franchisees still in start-up mode).
2. The data is difficult to obtain from their franchisees. Some franchisors don't require franchisees to report sales or operating expenses and don't have ways to collect this data.
3. They are afraid of getting sued.

If they choose to offer you this information, it will typically be presented in a document called the Uniform Franchise Offering

Circular (UFOC). At this point in the investigation, franchisors may or may not offer you the UFOC. Some will send the document and direct you to the earnings statement within it so you can better understand the predictable earnings power of the franchise. Others will require you to fill out their application form and be approved for a franchise prior to receiving this information.

We will briefly describe the components of a UFOC later in this chapter.

At the end of this first conversation, don't concern yourself with whether or not this is the right franchise for you, unless you are completely clear that it isn't.

After a successful first conversation, you will probably be left with one of four different experiences.

First is the feeling of "this isn't for me." If this is the case, communicate this to the franchisor and move on. State your reasons and give the franchisor a chance to respond, making sure your decision is based on real data, not a misperception on your part. Many franchise candidates pass up great opportunities based on misperceptions.

The second is a feeling of cautious optimism, a kind of "so far, so good" feeling. While the first conversation was successful, you aren't jumping to any conclusions right now. You are merely focused on what both you and the franchisor have determined are the next steps.

The third feeling is an adrenaline rush. You may be left pumped up thinking, "When do I get started?" Cool your heels and take a step back. You only have the headlines, not the details. You don't know enough to determine whether or not this is the right opportunity for you. Just as a person coming off a successful first date isn't wise to jump a plane, head to Vegas, grab the first Elvis impersonator they see for their witness, and get married, it isn't wise for you to mentally purchase a franchise after one conversation. Create some distance between yourself and your emotions. While contagious enthusiasm is a good thing, right now *cautious optimism is a better thing.*

Lastly, fear. This kind of fear is merely F.E.A.R, meaning *false emotions appearing real.* What's there to be afraid of? You just had a conversation. You didn't make any commitments other than to possibly take one more step in the process. Nobody is trying to lift your wallet or steal your purse. Give yourself permission to be afraid and then honor your commitment (if you made one) to take the next step in the process.

Congratulations. You've just successfully completed step one. Only five more steps left to a "yes" or "no" decision.

Step Two: Qualification

At this point, many franchisors will ask you to fill out a copy of their application form. Application forms are often called such things as confidential questionnaires, qualification forms, approval forms, or a host of other names. They generally request much of the following information:

- Name, address, contact information
- Work history (or they will ask you to attach a resume)
- Personal financial statement (summary)
- Earnings history
- Monthly expense budget (to see what it takes to run your household)
- Education history
- Goals and objectives
- Location/area preferences
- Strengths and weaknesses

Additionally, some franchisors will ask behavior-based questions relevant to the running of their business, such as:

- What is your management style?
- How do you solve problems?
- How many people can you effectively manage?
- Are you a people person?
- How are you at managing our type of employees?
- How are you at servicing our type of customer?
- Picture yourself in our establishment. What do you think a typical franchisee's day is like? Would you enjoy a day like that?
- Are you looking to go home for dinner every night or do you leave only after the job is done?
- Are you comfortable with risk?
- Do you see yourself as passionate about what we do?

It's in your best interest to be open and honest about this information. Skilled franchisors will evaluate you against their profile of a successful franchisee. Where puffery or inflating your credentials may help you get a higher paying job, if you're not feeding the franchisor factual information, your chance of survival, if selected as a franchisee, has just been reduced. You want to know exactly which of your skills is and isn't relevant. You want to know exactly what you already have in place that can propel you forward as well as what you're missing. Shoot straight and be generous with information and franchisors will generally respond in kind.

Keep in mind, you're not obligating yourself to purchase a franchise by simply filling out these forms. Also remember that the franchisor isn't obligated to offer you one either. These forms are for information gathering purposes only. Franchisors should use this information to help them determine, from their perspective, whether or not you match their profile of a successful franchisee.

Some franchisors will ask you to divulge such things as Social Security numbers, banking account numbers, brokerage account numbers, and other detailed financial information. At this stage, they really don't need this type of information. While many franchisors' forms ask for this data, generally franchisors are OK if you leave this information blank for now. Typically, they aren't going to run credit reports or validate banking and brokerage account balances until they're ready to either invite you into their office or offer you a franchise.

You might be afraid to provide such personal information. You may be thinking, "I'll provide it once I'm sure I'm going to buy the franchise." Remember, you aren't *entitled* to own a franchise. A skilled franchisor is going make sure you are *qualified*. A franchisor can disqualify you for any reason. Skilled franchisors are going to evaluate you with the same level of diligence you're going to evaluate them. If a franchisor finds you standoffish or closed-minded, they may think, "This candidate isn't a win-win person," and decline to offer you a franchise. Just because you have the money doesn't mean you're guaranteed an approval. Skilled franchisors are going to make sure you have the necessary KASH. Remember, "A" stands for "Attitude." If you aren't a win-win, problem-solving person, the competent franchisors you would want to do business with are going to walk away from you.

You might also be afraid to provide this information because you don't know who you're talking to or what they'll do with it. You might think your financial statement is going to be splashed all over cyberspace or the franchisor is going to sign you up to receive spam from online retailers. Perhaps there are exceptions, but usually the only people who will see your information are those who would need to see it, such as the franchise salesperson and others evaluating you as a candidate. At the end of the process (usually after step four), if you ask to be considered, many franchisors have formal or informal committees consisting of the department heads of franchise operations, franchise sales, and executive leadership such as the CEO and COO. These committees will verify your financial statement, run a credit report, and check personal references. However, this generally occurs much later in the process.

Step two is almost all about you. A skilled franchisor is going to prepare for this meeting by reviewing your qualifications and comparing your background, skills, attributes, and capitalization against their profile for a successful franchisee. They will identify what you're missing, bring it to your attention, and ask you questions to determine whether or not you're willing to do what it takes.

For instance, they may say, "I see you don't have direct sales experience. In this business you need to spend at least ten hours a week networking for leads and cold-calling customers. This responsibility falls to the owner. Is this something you are willing to do? Is this a skill you're willing to master?"

Franchisors will go into this meeting trying to determine with a high degree of accuracy whether or not, from their perspective, you're a match. They will dig deep into your background, trying to understand how your skills will transfer into your new business. They will ask financial questions to determine whether or not you can access the capital necessary to sustain your franchise operation until it's profitable while at the same time meeting your family obligations.

They will also give you an opportunity to ask them questions to fill in your information gaps. This meeting is a simple give-and-take of information, with you mostly on the "give" side of the equation. This isn't a bad thing. If the franchisor you're working with possesses both skills and integrity, they will spot a potential match before you do. At the end of the conversation, don't be afraid to ask questions like, Mr. Franchisor ...

- What do you see as my transferable skills? How do these skills relate to your business?
- How do I compare against the profile of a successful franchisee? What do I have to offer? What am I missing? How will you support me in these areas?
- Knowing what you know now, where would you predict I might struggle?
- How do you see me achieving my goals with your franchise?
- What concerns do you have?
- If you had to make a decision on me now, would you approve me as a franchisee? Why or why not?
- Given my existing skills and experience, what role do you see me playing in this business?
- Assuming I want to hire around my weaknesses, what type of person would I need to hire? What skills would they need to possess? What role would they play in my business?
- Am I a culture fit for your franchise?
- What can I always count on the franchisor for?
- What do you count on the franchisees for?

At the end of the second meeting, although a franchisor may not offer you official approval, any skilled franchisor representative who isn't supremely confident you'll eventually be approved, will either end your investigation process or stall it in order to tell you what you're missing and give you the opportunity to provide it. For instance, you might be missing basic computer skills, which may disqualify you as a franchisee. A skilled, high-integrity franchisor may ask you to take some computer classes and then invite you back into the process once you offer some proof of completion, such as a certificate.

At this point, you will have gone through two interviews and the experience of being thoroughly interviewed and screened. You should have the experience of having to earn the franchise the same way you would have to earn an attractive job offer. If you're not getting the experience of having to earn the franchise, beware. Some franchisors are so eager to grow, they may offer franchises to people who they wouldn't hire to run the same business.

If you are having the experience of having to earn a franchise, this still doesn't mean you are working with a reputable franchisor. Do a quick gut check to see which of two feelings you're experiencing.

1. You will feel that the franchisor is making a genuine effort to get to know you. You'll feel like they are listening for what you want your life to look like, and if they can't produce your desired results, you would expect them to tell you.

2. You will feel like you're "being sleazed." The franchisor has said, "Not everyone will be awarded a franchise," or "You better keep the process moving forward because we have other candidates looking at the same area." In sales, they call this "doing a take-away." The franchisor representative is merely testing you to see whether or not you are a viable buyer or if you're wasting their time.

At the end of the second meeting, evaluate whether or not you want to take the next step in the process. Don't worry about having to someday write the franchisor a big check. That day isn't today. Skilled franchisors aren't going to put any pressure on you at this point to make any decisions. Some franchise sales representatives may ask you questions such as, "If you had to make a decision right now, what would it be?" Answer however you choose to answer. If you get the feeling that the franchisor representative is looking at you like a commission check rather than a person, make note of it. Or they may simply be trying to find what issues you have so they can help you gather the information you need.

If the franchise recruiter seems overly anxious, it could mean they are simply happy to have you in their pipeline. Only 10 to 20 percent of people who request information about a franchise actually fill out an application. Although filling out applications only takes an hour or two and obligates you to nothing, franchisors recognize that it's a big emotional step to take. You have moved one step closer to designing your life and career. They pay attention to people like you. In the eyes of the franchisor, you have elevated yourself from the 99 percent who don't do anything to the 10 to 20 percent who have taken at least one bold step of committed action and have the potential of being the 1 percent who will join their franchise system.

Step Three: Reviewing the UFOC and Franchise Agreements

After two conversations, whether face-to-face or over the phone, the franchisor will typically send you their Uniform Franchise Offering Circular, or UFOC. The UFOC is the document that defines the legal relationship between the franchisor and franchisees. But the relationship between franchisees and solid and reputable franchisors extends beyond the confines of a legal relationship and develops into deeply committed personal relationships. These relationships transcend their obligations outlined in the UFOC and franchise agreements. When franchisees and franchisors (or their respective attorneys) pull out the franchise agreement as a means to define their relationship, it's because the relationship has been damaged and the trust has been violated.

Although it may not be described in these exact words in the UFOC, the roles and responsibilities of the franchisor are:

- To do whatever it takes (within reason) to give you the tools necessary to win
- To maintain the integrity of the brand

The roles and responsibilities of franchisees are equally simple:

- To master the franchisor's business model
- To deliver their products and services to your customers to the best of your ability, consistent with the spirit and intent of the franchisor
- To maintain the integrity of the brand

Franchisees' profitability is the lifeblood of any franchise organization. If franchisees aren't profitable, the franchise system eventually collapses like a house of cards. There's no other way to build a successful franchise system other than by building on the successes of profitable franchisees.

However, no franchisor is going to expressly state in a franchise agreement that it's their responsibility to help make you profitable. They are going to place the responsibility squarely on your shoulders and absolve themselves of any legal responsibility if you lose. Even in the best franchise systems, not every franchisee wins. In our litigious society, the franchisor must protect both their investment and the investments of other franchisees. They do this by promising you little in the way of support in writing. That way if the relationship sours and you take them to court, as long as they delivered on the minimal commitments they were obligated to perform under the franchise agreement, they win. Franchise agreements are written so the franchisor wins and you lose. While at first this may seem unfair, remember that the franchisor has an obligation to protect the entire franchise system, which requires such an imbalance.

The other franchisees are counting on the franchisor to survive. Franchisors must design a franchise agreement that ensures that no one franchisee can take down the entire system. Franchise agreements are written to reflect the litigious times we live in. Simply because a franchisor promises you little doesn't mean they deliver you little. Competent franchisors regularly and routinely offer franchisees assistance and services beyond what's required under the franchise agreement.

The simple truth is if you go into the legal departments of most skilled franchisors, you can tell which file cabinets hold the franchise agreements. They're the ones with the most dust on them because those cabinets are seldom opened and those agreements seldom read. Why? Because franchisors know their survival is completely dependent on whether or not you and the other franchisees win. They're willing to do whatever it takes (within reason and budget constraints), regardless of what their agreement says or doesn't say.

We're not saying, "Don't read your agreement." You have to be aware of what your agreement does and doesn't say. We're saying the only time to concern yourself with what your agreement says is when your committed personal relationship has failed.

In this section we're only going to touch on what to look for within the UFOC. There are many articles available on the web or in publications such as *FTC Guidelines to Buying a Franchise*, which can be accessed at www.franchise.org.

All Uniform Franchise Offering Circulars follow the same format, mandated by federal and state regulators. They all consist of 23 items, plus any exhibits and appendixes the franchisor includes. We will briefly describe what those 23 items are and what to look for as you conduct a *business* review. We recommend you hire a franchise attorney to do a thorough *legal* review. You'll find a comprehensive list of franchise attorneys on the International Franchise Association web site, www.franchise.org. Click on the tab for "suppliers" and you'll find a section for attorneys.

Many attorneys will tell you they know something about franchising and are perfectly capable of reviewing a UFOC. Franchising is a highly nuanced business, and unless an attorney specializes in the topic, he or she won't know the ins and outs of franchising and what franchisors will and won't do. It's been our experience that franchise candidates who hire attorneys outside of franchising receive pages and pages of copious legal notes, high legal bills because the attorneys don't know what to look for, and in the end, don't get the expert advice they paid for.

Item 1: The Franchisor, Its Predecessors, and Affiliates

This will give you a brief history of the franchisor, how it came to be, and what business they are in.

What to Look Out For. Realize that it takes five years to master anything. If a franchisor has less than five years operating their business model, this dramatically increases your risk. They may be testing their model with your money. However, if the franchisor's key executives have substantial experience in a similar business, your risk may be lessened. For instance, many fine executives of national franchise systems or other chains break away and start their own franchises.

Item 2: Corporate Officers and Business Experience

This section offers you background on the decison makers.

What to Look Out For

- Do the officers have franchise experience? Have they grown other franchise chains before? If so, how successful are these past chains now? Did these executives move on to another challenge after giving the chain stability or jump ship after they ran aground? Franchising is often described as a closed society. Many franchise professionals bounce around from company to company because companies look for experienced franchise executives. Keep in mind "experience" doesn't always mean "competent."

Item 3: Litigation

Pay attention to this section. Franchisors need to disclose in this section which people (identified in Item 2) have pending civil, criminal, or other actions alleging violations of franchising, antitrust, securities law, and unfair or deceptive trade practices. They have to disclose a full ten-year history of such activity. Be mindful we live in a highly litigious society, so some legal disputes are normal and acceptable. A recent poll of franchise attorneys and experts taken by The Franchise Performance Group showed that 50 percent of those polled thought it was acceptable if a franchisor has 1 percent or less of their franchisees engaged in some form of litigation. For instance, if a franchisor has 100 active franchisees and has one case of litigation (past or pending), this is normal. Another group of franchise attorneys and experts stated that you should look more at the nature and severity of the litigation rather than the percentage. Either way, litigation is an indicator of a breakdown in the franchisee-franchisor relationship. Even if the franchisor is winning these cases, be cautious. The agreement is designed so they win. Read these litigation cases and see what the franchisees are alleging.

Item 4: Bankruptcy

Affiliates, predecessors, partners, and officers must disclose, over a ten-year period, any personal bankruptcies and bankruptcies of companies they owned or were officers in or if they declared bankruptcy within 12 months after their tenure as an officer. While bankruptcies are more common and less stigmatized now than in the past, still pay attention. In a bankruptcy, someone who is supposed to be getting paid isn't. While the people declaring bankruptcy may have followed the proper legal processes to discharge their payment obligations to pay their creditors, you have to determine whether or not they have discharged their moral obligation to honor their commitments. Why is this important? Franchisors typically promise you little in their written franchise agreement. The success of a franchisee-franchisor relationship transcends any legal obligations that exist. It's built on a foundation of morality, integrity, ethics, and trust. Bankruptcy is a legal maneuver to cancel personal and corporate commitments and obligations. What is legal isn't always moral. If they used the legal system to cancel their commitments to others in the past, it's possible they will do the same to you in the future.

Even if no moral issue exists, bankruptcy is usually a clear sign of business failure. The past, left unchecked, has a way of repeating itself. Find out what the officers or people involved learned from their bankruptcy. Unless they have put measures in place to prohibit this from ever happening again, be cautious. If you hear excuses outside of their control like, "the economy went south," or "competition was too fierce," think twice. Chances are there were plenty of companies doing business in the same economy with the same competitive pressures who didn't declare bankruptcy.

Regardless of whether the cause is integrity or skills, bankruptcy is a warning signal.

Item 5: Initial Franchise Fee

This section must include all the fees and payments to the franchisor required to open the business. If the franchise fee is not uniform, such as in different fees for larger or smaller territories, the franchisor needs to disclose how these fees are determined. Most franchisors charge $25,000 to $40,000 in franchise fees for single-unit territories, which may or may not provide a protected territory. Many franchisors will discount franchise fees, typically 20 to 30 percent, if franchisees invest in three units or territories or more upfront.

Beware of franchisors who take large franchise fees, over $40,000, upfront. Franchisors who do this understand they are priced higher than what most franchisors charge. If they provide a higher level of support than most franchisors, this can actually be a bonus. Sometimes franchisors will charge a higher franchise fee if their business model produces exceptionally high financial returns. As long as franchisees are producing strong financial results, a higher fee may be justified.

However, some franchisors may charge more if they think the market will bear it. Beware of these. They may be more concerned with taking your cash upfront and less concerned with your success over the long haul.

Item 6: Other Fees

Franchisors must disclose all recurring fees or payments that franchisees pay the franchisor and affiliates. They must also disclose how they compute those fees.

Those fees are typically:

1. **Royalties.** Royalties are the lifeblood of any franchise organization. Royalty rates fluctuate depending on the size, the nature of the business, the level of ongoing support, and financial returns. Most franchisors in the service, retail, and food sectors charge 4 to 8 percent. However, there are currently over 70 different industries represented in franchising and different industries have different norms.

2. **Local advertising.** Many franchisors will stipulate a minimum level of expenditures for advertising. Some will direct which advertising vehicles you must use, such as direct mail or Yellow Page advertising.

3. **National (or regional) ad fund.** Since the vast majority of franchisors in the United States have less than 100 units, and, depending on the type of business, it can take 600 units or more to have the critical mass necessary to be able to afford national advertising to reach all the customers, some national ad funds may not be able to effectively market the brand. Find out if some of these funds are used to offset the salaries and expenses of the franchisor's marketing department, for instance, the salaries and expenses which should be covered by your royalty contributions. If the franchise you're looking to join has the necessary critical mass within the United States or within a region to benefit from mass media, radio and television advertising, these funds can offer franchisees substantial value. Where no such critical mass exists, these funds may offer little value beyond ego gratification to the franchisees and could be considered a second royalty. How much a franchisor charges and where these funds are allocated speaks volumes about the competency and integrity level of the franchisor. Skilled, high-integrity franchisors will want you to target your advertising dollars where they are best spent to drive brand awareness and customer trial, regardless if it's on the local, regional, or national level. If they can create leverage by co-

oping the advertising expenditures of their franchisees on a regional or national level in order to create substantial buying power, it's in everyone's best interest that they do so. And responsible franchisors will. Look closely at how this money is collected and where this money is spent.

4. **Transfer fees.** Franchisors will charge you a nominal fee, generally less than the franchise fee to train and develop the future purchaser of your business. This is of great benefit to franchisees because once they sell their business, the franchisor will help with the training, development, and transition of the new owner. The seller is then free to focus on their next step.

5. **Renewal fees.** At the end of the term of your franchise agreement, franchisors charge a nominal fee to renew the agreement for another term. A typical franchise has a ten-year agreement and a ten-year renewal option. Renewal fees are typically less than the cost of a new franchise, usually 10 to 20 percent of the cost.

Item 7: The Initial Investment

Your total investment is broken down into categories such as franchise fee, equipment, leasehold improvements, inventory, grand opening advertising, pre-opening expenses such as travel and lodging for training, and working capital. You get to see where your money goes. You also get to see when the cash gets dispersed. In a typical franchise, aside from the franchise fee and some proprietary products most of this money will go to outside vendors and contractors. These expenditures do not represent a profit center to the franchisor.

Most skilled and high-integrity franchisors will do whatever it takes to help keep your front-end investment as low as possible so you don't deplete your cash and to increase your chances for survival.

The one cost franchisors have a tendency to underestimate is the amount of working capital that's needed. Working capital is the cash you need to inject into the business to cover operating costs until the revenues generated can cover all your costs and you reach your break-even point. The Federal Trade Commission only requires franchisors to disclose *three months* of working capital. Since many businesses do not break even until after six to twelve months and some even longer, this number can be misleading. Make sure you know how long it takes to break even so you possess enough working capital.

Item 8: Restrictions on Sources of Products and Services

Franchisors must disclose your obligations to purchase products and services from the franchisor, affiliates, or approved suppliers.

It's reasonable for a franchisor to mandate who a franchisee purchases from to maintain consistency and quality. However, talk to other franchisees to make sure these products are reasonably priced with reasonable terms and can't be purchased elsewhere at a lower price. Some franchisors will generate revenue from your purchases in the form of rebates from the supplier. They will negotiate an attractive national price and then keep a percentage of the savings for themselves. While not entirely bad, negotiating best prices is a service skilled franchisors offer franchisees as part of the value of their royalties. These franchisors will often pass the entire cost savings along to the franchisees. A rebate may be justified in lieu of lower royalties. There are companies who have no royalties and depend on profits from franchisees' direct purchases or rebates from other suppliers for their revenues.

If you take a step back you can see the different ways unskilled or low-integrity franchisors can put their hand in your pocket without your knowing exactly how much is being taken. Those ways include:

- Royalties
- National ad funds
- Rebates from your purchases from their approved vendors which could go to you

High-integrity and highly skilled franchisors will fully disclose and want you to know what your investment is now and in the future without hidden or hard-to-calculate fees or surcharges. They will take their money in royalty payments or in other disclosed ways. For those high-integrity franchisors who sell proprietary products and services, they will take reasonable markups and offer you reasonable terms. They will disclose what those markups are.

Item 9: Franchisee's Obligations

You will receive a detailed list of everything you'll be held responsible for including, but not limited to, such things as:

- Purchases
- Initial and ongoing training
- Compliance standards
- Restrictions
- Warranties
- Quotas or minimum performance levels
- Fees
- Insurance
- Advertising minimums
- Staffing requirements
- Submitting to inspections and audits
- Recordkeeping
- Dispute resolution

Since this is a legal document, this section can be dense. It can also appear very threatening. Don't be spooked by the language. The franchisors are protecting both their interests and the interests of the other franchisees. They make sure their agreements have plenty of teeth in case they are ever forced to protect the brand. You want to do business with a franchisor who has a solid reputation with its franchisees for win-win problem solving. When a problem or disagreement occurs, they don't go into their file cabinet, pull out your agreement, and force you into unwilling compliance. They listen to your issues, clearly state their issues in return, and craft solutions where both parties can get the most of what they want. When you start interviewing franchisees in step four of this six-step process, you'll learn how to identify these franchisors.

Item 10: Financing

Franchisors who offer franchisees direct financing will disclose the terms and conditions here. However, most franchisors will direct you to outside lenders and leasing companies and do not finance franchisees themselves.

Item 11: Franchisor's Obligations

The franchisor must disclose the services they will perform prior to your business opening such as:

- Training (location, duration, and subject matter)

- Site selection assistance/lease negotiation
- Construction assistance and design assistance
- Advertising
- Permitting
- Software support

Item 12: Territory

If the franchisor offers protected territories or territory restrictions, how they determine territory descriptions and what those restrictions are will be spelled out here. Your actual territory description will appear in your franchise agreement.

We hear sad stories in the media about struggling franchisees from prominent fast-food chains who feel they are too close together and competing for the same customers. This is why having a protected territory is such an important issue. Ideally, franchisors and franchisees would like to do business in a wide enough area so they don't butt heads with each other. At the same time, the area needs to be small enough to prevent the competition from staking a claim and camping out at your borders. Franchisees often come from the place, "Sure, I want to grow the chain, but not in my backyard." They feel threatened by another franchisee coming into their geographic area, even in a noncontiguous trade area, thinking, "This new franchisee will restrict my ability to grow in the future." Franchisors, on the other hand, want to keep the territories small to gain critical mass, dominate the market, and outpace their competition. Because of this dynamic, many times franchises won't achieve the same critical mass another, dominant, nonfranchise chain such as Starbucks® has achieved. That's why Starbucks® chose to expand through company-owned stores. Threats from franchisee litigation would have doomed the "Starbucks® on every corner" strategy. When negotiating a territory, trust and open communication become critical. Do business with a franchisor who will offer you territory protection or are convinced you will succeed without one.

Some franchisors reserve the right to open company outlets within your territory, operating under the same brand name or, perhaps, under a different brand name. Their thinking is if you aren't upholding the standards of the brand, then they can open up in your territory and protect their interests. This also gives them the legal right to steal your brand equity if you're a top performer. Few franchisors would ever consider doing this, but may still reserve the right. Franchisors who have other protections under their franchise agreement typically don't need this right to protect their brand. If you cannot negotiate this out of your franchise agreement, think carefully about proceeding any further.

Item 13: Trademarks

Franchisors must disclose which trademarks, service marks, names, logos, and symbols they use to identify the franchise business. They must also disclose if these are registered with the United States Patent and Trademark Office, the corresponding dates of registration, and proper identification numbers. If franchisees won't have such protection, the franchisor must disclose this lack of protection.

If a franchisor cannot protect its trademarks, then it's entirely possible you can build your brand and have a competitor come into the same market and advertise to your customers, using your name, logo, or slogans. Any franchisor who cannot protect its brand isn't a franchisor you want to sink your money into.

Item 14: Patents, Copyrights, and Proprietary Information

If a franchisor owns patents or copyrights, they must be disclosed here. Franchisors will often make general references to their proprietary business systems and trade secrets in this section. If a franchisor doesn't own patents or copyrights, it might be OK depending on the industry. For instance, a residential cleaning franchise such as Molly Maids® may use the same vacuum cleaners as other competitors, but the power of their franchise system isn't dependent on the proprietary technology of their vacuums. Their genius is in how they find, manage, and retain good help, satisfy existing customers, and market for new customers. Other chains, like Lawn Doctor®, a large national lawn service business, have proprietary equipment and chemicals, which gives them a competitive advantage in the marketplace and adds value to their system.

Item 15: Obligation to Participate in the Actual Operation of the Franchise Business

If a franchisor is going to require you to work full-time in the business, it will be disclosed here. Many franchisors require you to work full-time in the business, putting forth your best efforts in the early stages so your business makes it and your investment is protected. Other franchisors, such as Sport Clips®, a national hair care franchise, want you to keep your job or other business interests so you can plow all your cash flow back into their business in order to accelerate your growth.

Item 16: Restrictions on What a Franchisee May Sell

Franchisors must describe your obligations to sell only the goods and services they approve of. They must also disclose any restrictions they will impose on the customers you can sell to.

Item 17: Renewal, Termination, Transfer, and Dispute Resolution

Franchisors will present a table that will identify the following:

- The length of term of the franchise
- Renewal or extension terms
- Requirements for a franchisee to renew or extend
- How a franchisee can terminate their agreement. Many franchisors don't give franchisees the right to terminate their agreement. They expect them to sell the franchise to a new owner in order to protect their royalty stream. This is normal and acceptable. This also prevents a successful franchisee from suddenly taking down the franchisor's brand, putting up their own brand and omitting royalty payments.
- How the franchisor can terminate their agreement without cause. Pay particular attention to this section. Most franchisors do not reserve any right to terminate your agreement without cause. It's not normal nor is it generally acceptable for a franchisor to reserve this right.
- How the franchisor can terminate their agreement with cause. For instance, a franchisee may be selling unauthorized, infe-

rior products to their customers. A franchisor may default them as a result. As long as the products are removed from the store within an agreed-upon timeframe, the franchisee will be marked back in compliance. If they refuse, they run the risk of having their agreement terminated.

- "Noncurable" franchisee defaults, meaning a franchisee has no opportunity to correct a problem and it results in grounds for the immediate termination of their franchise agreement. For instance, if a franchisee is convicted of a felony, this may allow a franchisor to immediately terminate their franchise agreement. As long as a guilty verdict is reached, a franchisor may reserve the right to protect their brand and move swiftly by terminating the agreement without further hearing. This is normal and reasonable.
- Franchisee's obligations upon nonrenewal or termination. If a franchisee elects not to continue in their business or is terminated, they may have certain obligations such as taking down signs, turning in their confidential operations manual and proprietary marketing materials, and paying outstanding balances.
- Assignment of contract by franchisor. Franchisors will typically reserve the right to sell their own business and assign their obligations to the acquiring party. This is normal and acceptable.
- How to transfer your business. Franchisors will discuss acceptable methods of selling your business to a third party. They will typically reserve the right to approve who you are selling to and require the new buyer to go through their training programs. Most franchisors will charge you a transfer fee to cover their expenses to train and support the new owner. Some franchisors will reserve a first right of refusal to purchase your business. In other words, you may receive an offer from someone who wants to purchase your business for $100,000 cash. A franchisor may reserve a window of opportunity to purchase your business for the same $100,000 cash.
- What will occur if you die or become disabled and are incapable of running the business. Franchisors will typically give your heirs or estate six months or so to sell the business to a new owner.

- Noncompete clauses during the term of the franchise agreement and after the agreement expires, is terminated, or you sell your franchise.
- Modification of your agreement. This agreement details the steps you and the franchisor must take if you both agree to modify your franchise agreement in any way.
- Dispute resolution. Some franchisors will restrict how you resolve disputes. For instance, many franchisors require you to waive trial by jury and resolve your conflicts through binding arbitration. Some franchisors even require that you present your case first to a panel of fellow franchisees and key employees of the franchisor. In case of legal action, many franchisors will require you to resolve your dispute in the state in which they're located and under the jurisdiction of their state laws. Usually this means travel expenses and additional attorney's fees on your part, increasing your motivation to try to resolve these issues outside of costly court battles. This is normal and typical.

Item 18: Public Figures

Franchisors need to disclose any financial arrangements they have with public figures in the use of their franchise name or symbols. Franchisors using public figures in this capacity run a high risk. For instance, at one time Kenny Roger's Roasters® was a very popular and high-growth, quick-service restaurant chain. Then Kenny Rogers got caught up in a highly publicized scandal, which tarnished his image and that of the franchise brand. We recommend you carefully consider the risks of doing business with any franchisors that are attached to high-profile people, such as sports figures, politicians, or celebrities.

Item 19: Earnings Statements

If a franchisor makes an earnings claim, they will be in this section. Many franchisors fear the legal risk and simply don't do it. However, more and more franchisors are honoring the requests of franchise candidates who want this information. Over time we predict most franchisors will get over their fear of being sued and disclose this information.

Item 20: List of Outlets

Here you'll find an updated owners list, giving you the street addresses of the franchise locations, as well as the franchisees' names and phone numbers for you to contact.

Additionally, franchisors must disclose the names of franchisees, who over the last three years, sold their franchise, had their franchise terminated or not renewed, were bought out by the franchisor, or have failed.

If a franchisor has a high failure rate, listen to the reasons why. If you hear them put the responsibility on the franchisees by making comments like, "Well, if the franchisees would have followed the system, they wouldn't have failed," keep probing. Isn't the franchisor responsible for bringing the franchisees into the system? Isn't the franchisor responsible for training and developing franchisees on their systems and holding them accountable for executing their business strategy? Doesn't the franchisor share equally in the responsibility of the franchisees' failure? Ask follow-up questions like, "What is it about your recruiting methods that you're bringing in the wrong people?" and "What is it about your operating system that so many franchisees are refusing to, or unable to, execute it properly?" If you see franchisors absolving themselves of responsibility for their franchisees' poor performance, then chances are if you struggle, they won't know how to help you, either. Inexperienced or unsophisticated franchisors look at franchisees' failures as just that — franchisees' failures. They look at franchisees' victories as the system is working. They take ownership of the victories and absolve themselves of responsibility for their losses. Consider eliminating them from consideration.

Top-quality, responsible franchisors see the franchise network as one body consisting of the franchisor, franchisees, and perhaps even suppliers. If one member suffers, then the body suffers. If one member wins, the body rejoices. Franchisee victories are their victories and franchisee failures are their failures too.

It's normal and predictable for a mature franchisor, defined as ten years as a franchisor or more, to have more than 15 percent of their franchises for sale. Many franchisees keep their business roughly seven to ten years. As you call franchisees, if you get a sense that more than 15 percent of franchisees are selling, this may be an indicator of a problem. Something may not be working within the system and disgruntled franchisees want out.

Item 21: Financial Statements

Franchisors must disclose audited financial statements in accordance with generally accepted accounting principles, and balance sheets. If you don't know how to read a financial statement, bring this section to an accountant for review. Pay particular attention to items such as:

- **Cash on hand.** The lower the cash balance, the more temptation a franchisor has to sell you a franchise and build their cash reserves.
- **Long-term debt.** Make sure the franchisor isn't so heavily financed they can't reinvest back into their system.
- **Cash flow.** Make sure the franchisor is cash-flow positive, or in the case of a new franchisor, is on track to become cash-flow positive shortly.
- **Balance sheet.** Make sure the franchisor has assets in the company and has something at stake. Some franchisors show statements with fewer assets or net worth than the investment level they require franchisees to make. This is upside down. Franchisors should have as much or more at stake than franchisees.

Item 22: Contracts

Franchisors will provide copies of all documents you are required to sign in this section, including the franchise agreements, lease or financing agreements, etc. The terms of the franchise agreement should accurately reflect what is stated in the UFOC.

Item 23: Receipt

This document you sign stating that you acknowledge receiving the UFOC. Signing this document obligates you to nothing.

Read your UFOC, keeping these points in mind. Highlight anything in the UFOC that appears off, that you're uncomfortable with, or that you simply cannot agree to. Make an appointment to review these with the franchise recruiter. After you review your issues with the franchisor, you will be usually left with one of three feelings:

1. I'm OK.
2. I'm not OK, but it's OK that I'm not OK.
3. I'm not OK, and it's not OK that I'm not OK.

If you aren't OK, the process ends here. Trust your "not OKness" as an indicator the franchise is not a match for you. If you're someone who has looked at five or more opportunities and have come to the same place each time, take a look at the reasons why. If you see consistent patterns across different franchise opportunities, perhaps franchising isn't for you. Or perhaps you're looking in the wrong sector. Remember, franchising operates in more than 70 different industries.

For everyone who is OK, it's time to start calling and, if possible, visiting franchisees to hear what they have to say.

Step Four: Franchisee Validation, Data Gathering, and Analysis

There is an old franchise joke which goes something like this.

What are five words no franchisee has ever heard?
"What is on your mind?"
Why? Many franchisees say what's on their mind before anyone asks!

Typically, getting a franchisee to open up is easy. You'll find them open and honest as it relates to answering all types of questions, including such financial information as, "How long does it take this business to break even?"

You must also remember that where they are in the lifecycle of their business colors the feedback they may give you. You have to read between the lines. For instance, if you're interviewing a franchisee deeply mired in the Grind and ask, "Knowing what you know now, would you make the same decision again?" you will have a stronger likelihood of hearing, "no," than at other times during the learning curve. It's the same as asking a pregnant mother in the midst of severe labor contractions whether or not she thinks having a baby was a good idea.

You may also get skewed feedback from franchisees in the Launch. Everything will seem just splendid, whether or not it really is.

When you're contacting franchisees, remember they have a business to run and time is their most precious resource. They are gifting you time the same way others donate money to charity. Respect their time by being prepared with questions. Don't take more than 15 or 20 minutes with any one franchisee. Franchisees have scores of candidates calling them all the time. Also, request an appointment. Just because you reach them by telephone or they're there when you stop in, doesn't mean it's a good time to talk. Find out when is the best time and remember to be flexible. Some franchisees may want to speak with you early in the day, before work begins and others will want to meet at night when work is over. Regardless of the franchise they're in, they will only have certain hours in which to generate revenue and may not want to be interviewed during these hours. Respect their time by not wasting it schmoozing. They know this stage in your investigation because they've been through it. Prepare your questions in advance, stick to your outline, ask the questions you prepared, then hang up the phone or leave their place of business. Be quick and efficient, but get your questions answered.

And remember what you're interviewing for. "People don't buy drills, they buy holes." You don't want the franchise, you want the results. The purpose of every interview is to gather data to determine whether or not your "must have" and "wish to have" results will occur with this business with a high degree of probability.

When you start your interview, begin by getting some open-ended background information.

- What did you do before you invested in your franchise?
- What were your reasons for joining this franchise?
- How long have you been in business?
  - Franchisees with less than four months of experience are probably in the Launch. Unless they came into the franchise from a competitor or similar business, most of what they know about the business is simply theory. They haven't experienced all of what it takes to become successful. Most franchisees in the Launch are happy with their relationship with the franchisor. Asking a franchisee in the Launch, "How

do you like working with the franchisor?" is like asking a newlywed on their honeymoon, "How do you like being married to your spouse?" They can, however, offer you terrific information on the quality of the franchisor's training programs and guidance in getting a new business open.

- Ask, "Did the franchisor's training program adequately prepare you to launch your business? If not, what was missing?"
- "Did the franchisor adequately direct you during the pre-opening process, helping you stay organized and knowing what to do and when? If not, what was missing?"
- "Did the franchisor's grand opening strategy work? If not, what was missing? What would you do differently?"

■ Realize that franchisees who have been open four months to two years may be in some version of the Grind. While it's reasonable to assume they may be negative about the choice they made because of underestimating the level of effort involved or other issues, you can still gather insights into the skill level of the franchisor. Remember, franchisees in the Grind need high levels of franchisor interaction, plenty of coaching, training, and consulting. They should be in constant contact with the franchisor.

- Ask, "How often are you in contact with the franchisor?"
- "What support are you getting to help you get your business to the next level?"
- "What more could the franchisor be doing to help you win?"

Two of the best indicators of the competency level of any franchisor are:

- Franchisees' satisfaction with profitability
- Franchisees' satisfaction with the franchisee-franchisor relationship

We will look at each of these separately.

Determining Franchisees' Profitability

Even if a franchisee is relatively new in the business and may not be generating positive cash flow, you can ask them financial questions.

They should know the averages and norms. They should know both what a high-volume and low-volume franchise looks like. When asking financial questions it isn't important to ascertain how well each franchisee is doing financially. It's to determine *how well you will do financially*. Franchisees are less guarded and more apt to want to answer questions about the franchise system's norms and regional or national financial averages than about the results they are specifically generating. You can always ask whether or not their financial results are meeting their expectations.

Since most franchisees finance and operate their businesses differently, their financial statements may have wide variations. Some will more aggressively write-off expenses such as autos, trips, and medical insurance. Some will carry more debt than others. Some franchisees will pay themselves a salary, others will take no salary and pay themselves dividends. Some employ a manager and others are owner-operated. Your goal is to ask questions, which will give you consistent information. We recommend you get to what many franchisors call "total owner benefit." In other words, assuming franchisees take their entire benefit in one lump-sum, cash distribution at the end of the year, before debt, depreciation, amortization, paying the owner's salary and benefits, and aggressively writing off personal expenses, how much money would there be left for them to take home? Ask franchisees:

- What can a typical franchisee expect to make in gross sales and owner benefit in Year 1, 2, and 3 (before debt, depreciation, amortization, and before paying the owner a salary and benefits)?
  Year One: Gross sales_____ Owner benefit _____
  Year Two: Gross sales _____ Owner benefit_____
  Year Three: Gross sales _____ Owner benfit_____

- What would a high-volume franchisee make?
  Year One: Gross sales_____ Owner benefit_____
  Year Two: Gross sales _____ Owner benefit_____
  Year Three: Gross sales _____ Owner benefit_____

- What would a low-volume franchisee make?
  Year One: Gross_____ Owner benefit_____

Year Two: Gross _____ Owner benefit_____
Year Three: Gross_____ Owner benefit_____

The three largest, expense line items in any small business are: cost of sales, cost of labor, and total occupancy costs, for those franchises which require an office or storefront. "Total occupancy" is a common real estate term, which includes the cost of rent, and the renter's pro-rated share of insurance, common area maintenance, and taxes on the building. Depending on the franchise opportunity, cost of sales, labor, and occupancy added together represent 65 to 80 percent of the franchisees' entire cost of doing business. Make sure you receive consistent information regarding these cost areas as they represent the lion's share of the franchisees' expenses.

Ask the franchisees for typical operating cost information such as:

- As a percentage of sales, what should my cost of sales be?
- As a percentage of sales, what should my cost of labor be?
- As a percentage of sales, what should my total occupancy cost be?

Keep in mind, if you're investigating a business that required a retail storefront or office, your rent will probably be a predictable fixed amount each month, not a percentage of your sales. However, by asking franchisees, "As a percentage of sales, what should my total occupancy cost be?" you will hear what you can effectively budget for rent payment. As you look into local rental rates, you will know if the average sales volume will justify the cost of what you'll be required to pay in rent.

Some franchisors will assist your information-gathering exercise by providing you with simple, blank financial statements that you can use as a template to help you gather accurate financial data. Others will publish this data in Item 19 in their UFOC. Still others, possibly afraid of future potential lawsuits, will offer no assistance.

For those who need help gathering the elements of what goes into a business plan, there are many resources available. You can go to your local office of the Small Business Administration (SBA), Small Business Development Center (SBDC), or Service Corps of Retired Executives (SCORE). You can find your local office by visiting their web sites.

- www.sba.gov
- www.sbdc.gov
- www.score.org

There are software packages you can purchase, like Business Plan Pro, that will walk you step-by-step through how to write a business plan. For those who need additional hand-holding, you can also get the assistance of a Certified Public Accountant (CPA) to help you analyze the data you gather.

Ask the franchisor to help you determine the KASH model of success (described in Chapter 6).

- What does it take to succeed?
- What skills do I need to develop in order to win?
- What activities do I need to be doing every day to produce outstanding results?
- What are the most common mistakes new franchisees make in this business?
- What advice would you give a new franchisee who's starting out?
- Where will I waste time if I'm not careful?

Determining Franchisees' Satisfaction Level

In Chapter 8, we discussed how the franchisee-franchisor relationship evolves over time, from new franchisees' total dependency on the franchisor during the Glee stage, to the franchisees' testing the boundaries of the relationship and asserting independence in the Me and Free stages, to eventually a win-win interdependent relationship characterized by the We stage, where each party is committed to the other's success.

Unskilled franchisors never make it to the We stage. Some get frozen either trying to control franchisees or to avoid being controlled by them. Others go too far in the other direction by not enforcing standards or ensuring quality and letting the franchisees do whatever they want.

Questions to Evaluate the Franchisee-Franchisor Relationship

- How would you describe your relationship with the franchisor?

- No matter what happens, what can you always count on the franchisor for?
- How has the franchisor's ongoing support made a difference in your business?
- What value are you receiving for your royalties? Is the advice and support you're receiving and the value of the brand worth the money you're investing in royalties?
- Knowing what you know now, would you make the same investment again?

Grading the Franchisor as a Franchisor

A peak-performing franchisor needs to show a high level of competency in four key areas:

1. Recruiting top-quality franchise candidates
2. Training, consulting, and coaching franchisees from the Launch into Winning or the Zone
3. Building powerful franchisee-franchisor relationships
4. Marketing and building the brand

Ask existing franchisees to grade the franchisor using a five-point rating scale in the following areas (1 representing failure and 5 representing excellence).

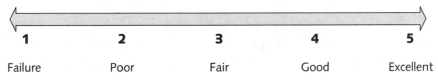

1	2	3	4	5
Failure	Poor	Fair	Good	Excellent

Ask, *"How would you rate the ..."*

- Franchisor's ability to recruit top-quality franchisees
- Value of the franchisor's initial training program
- Ability of support and field staff to identify and help fix franchisees' problems
- Value of ongoing training programs
- Value of field visits to franchisees' locations
- Value of national or regional meetings
- Ability of support staff to help develop franchisees' skills in critical areas of their business

- Franchisor's responsiveness to franchisees' issues and concerns
- Franchisor's track record for keeping their word and making good on their promises and commitments to the franchisees
- Quality of the relationship between the franchisees and the franchisor
- Leadership ability of the CEO and senior management
- CEO and senior management's vision of the future
- Value of the products and services being offered to the franchisees' customers
- Effectiveness of marketing and advertising programs
- Total effectiveness of the franchisor's business model to produce outstanding results

Any area in which a franchisor is rated from "failure" to "fair" ask one or two follow-up questions:

1. What is missing?
2. What could they be doing differently?

How Many Franchisees Should I Call?

There isn't any magic number of franchisees you should call. We recommend you speak to a minimum of five to ten franchisees, depending on the size of system, complexity of the operation, size of the investment, etc., simply to be able to identify trends and patterns and to see some consistency of information. After interviewing eight to ten franchisees, you should be hearing little new information, just confirmation of information you already have. Most franchisees will call five to ten franchisees before they make a decision as to whether or not they will visit the franchisor's home office and meet the company's officers and decision makers.

Your decision-making style will also play a role in how many franchisees you feel you need to contact. Referring back to Chapter 4, if you are an Action Hero or Comedian, you possess higher risk tolerance than most, and make "gut-based" or instinctive decisions rather than data-based ones. Since you typically err on the side of aggressiveness, play it safe and contact a few more than you think is necessary, just to unearth some information you may be missing before you decide whether or not you'll visit the franchisor's home office.

If you are a Faithful Sidekick or Private Eye, you make data-based decisions rather than emotional or instinctive decisions. You may want to contact most or all of the franchisees. You err on the side of caution. Since you are more risk-averse than most entrepreneurs, you may have a tendency to try to search out and discover the "magic" missing piece of data, which will complete the puzzle, guarantee your success, and alleviate your fears. This data however, probably doesn't exist. Once you contact eight to ten franchisees, the information you gather should be fairly consistent. You may feel like you don't have all the information you need to prepare for your visit to the home office, but this doesn't mean you don't have all the information. Your fear could be F.E.A.R., false experience appearing real. Two questions to continually ask yourself are:

- What information am I missing?
- If I had this information, how would it impact my investment decision?

Once you find yourself spending time gathering "nice to have" information, which won't impact your decision, it's time to stop gathering data. You may be engaging in "analysis paralysis," meaning gathering information in order to avoid making a decision.

Garbage In/Garbage Out

Computer programmers have an expression called GIGO, meaning "garbage in, garbage out." The quality of the output is only as good as the input. It's the same thing with franchising. The quality of information you receive from franchisees will be in direct relationship to the quality of the questions you ask. This is why this chapter frames some important questions for you. Remember, what you ask and what the franchisees hear may be two different things. Also remember that what they answer and what you hear may also be two different things. Take careful notes during and after your conversations.

For instance, a franchise candidate for a specialty retail franchise called a franchisee to ask how they were doing. The franchisee being called was running a high-volume store and had a quick start out of the blocks. The franchise candidate asked the franchisee, "What profits do you anticipate making at the end of the year?"

The franchisee thought quietly for a second, "Let's see," she thought. "After paying back my SBA loan, paying myself a salary, paying the expenses on my two cars, taking into account depreciation and amortization, I may not see a profit at the end of the year." Therefore the franchisee truthfully responded, "I don't expect to make any profits this year."

Now keep in mind, the object of a small business is not to make a profit because you get taxed on profits. The purpose is to generate cash flow and other financial benefits to the owner, such as equity build-up and write-offs. These are expenses that would otherwise have to be paid with after-tax dollars by those who have jobs instead of their own business. This includes such things as auto expenses and travel and entertainment (that is business related).

This particular franchisee was paying off the debt on her business and building equity, taking a salary, being aggressive with business expenses, but not showing a profit. She was however, meeting her financial objectives and succeeding in business. This point wasn't clearly articulated and the prospective franchisee missed it. As a matter of fact, the prospect hung up the phone thinking the franchisee was actually failing. The prospective franchisee missed out on a great franchise opportunity because he asked a garbage question and received a garbage answer.

Always check your understanding of what you heard. You might say, "Let me repeat what I just heard just to make sure I heard you correctly."

If the franchise candidate had used this technique and asked the franchisee, "If I heard you correctly, it sounds like your business is in trouble," the candidate would have received a different answer.

Analyzing Your Data

Remember, you don't want a franchise, you want results. A franchise is a vehicle that produces results. Ultimately, your data should be organized to help you determine whether or not your "must have" and much of your "wish to have" objectives can be achieved with an acceptable level of predictability. Ultimately, you want to determine if:

- The franchise business will produce your desired results.
- You are willing to do whatever it takes to acquire the KASH model of success.

- The franchisor will do whatever it takes to help you win.
- You have the necessary capital and you match the franchisor's profile of a successful franchisee.
- You are a culture fit for the organization.
- The franchisees and franchisor work together to help each other win.

We recommend creating a spreadsheet or a visual display like the following:

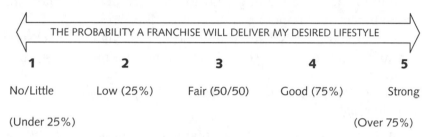

My "must have" objectives and by when I'm committed to accomplishing this.	Franchisor #1 What is the probability this will be achieved with this franchise?	Franchisor #2 What is the probability this will be achieved with this franchise?
My "wish to have" objectives and by when I'm committed to accomplishing this.	What is the probability this will be achieved with this franchise?	What is the probability this will be achieved with this franchise?

If all of your "must have" and most of your "wish to have" objectives will be met with a high degree of probability, the franchise brand is either strong or building, the franchisees are winning, the franchisee-franchisor relationship is intact, and you appear to be a culture fit for the organization, make an appointment with the franchisor's representative to visit the franchisor's home office. Your goal in visiting is to meet and interview the officers and decison makers. Some franchisors have some form of "Discovery Day," which other prospective franchisees may attend. Discovery Days are tightly organized in order to persuade and inform. The chance to talk to and listen to the concerns and questions of other prospective franchisees can be invaluable.

If any of these are missing, end the process here, and perhaps start the process with another franchisor.

We offer you a worksheet at the end of this chapter which will help you crystallize your observations and reach a proper decision.

Why Should I Spend the Money to Visit the Franchisor?

As of now, chances are you have only had telephone conversations or possibly one or two face-to-face meetings with the franchise recruiter. The opinions of one person may not accurately describe the reality of the franchisor or the franchise opportunity. Additionally, the franchise sales representative's compensation is typically not tied to whether or not you succeed in business, but to whether or not you sign a franchise agreement. Therefore, franchise salespeople have a tendency to overlook information, which may suggest future problems. It's imperative that you travel to the home office, look the decison makers in the eye and let them know who you are and what you're looking to accomplish. You're more likely to get straight feedback from the people who are held accountable for your success and whose problem you'll be if you don't succeed. You will learn things from visiting the franchisor's office that you can't learn any other way. Visiting the franchisor's office will either validate the information or opinions you have about the franchise being a solid investment and career opportunity, or you may discover new information which you find objectionable.

Step Five: Attending a Discovery Day or Visiting the Home Office

Many franchisors will set aside one or two days a month to host potential franchisees. While some may not have a Discovery Day as part of their franchisee recruitment process, if you ask to meet the decision makers, high-road franchisors understand what's at stake and will certainly oblige you.

High-Road Franchisors

Because both parties have so much at stake, the leadership teams of high-integrity and competent franchisors won't enter into a franchise agreement with anyone they haven't met. You risk your capital and they risk their corporate culture and the integrity of their brand. They will want to make sure you have an opportunity to thoroughly interview them and they will want to do the same with you. In the end you both want the same thing, to determine whether or not you fit the profile of a successful franchisee and whether your objectives can be met using their business model. Usually, at least half the day will be comprised of structured presentations to make sure you and others present receive consistent and accurate information about what it takes to win and what you can count on the franchisor for. The other half will be flexible; allowing you to ask whatever is on your mind. At the end of the day, you should have your questions answered and a realistic idea of what it takes to win and whether or not you fit in.

Anywhere from 50 to 80 percent of franchise candidates who attend a Discovery Day end up joining the franchise system they visit. For the remainder, either the candidate or the franchisor spots something which leads one of them to believe there isn't a match.

Low-Road Franchisors

Regardless of what they say, the picture the low-road franchisor has of you is one of a deposit slip with thousands of dollars written on it. They know if they can get in front of you, this will give them their greatest opportunity to close you. Discovery Day is code word for "Sales Close Day," meaning this is their big opportunity to reel you in. The day will be an eight-hour commercial about how great their opportunity is and how lucky you are if you are "chosen" to be part of it. Of course to be chosen, all you need to do is be able to fog a mirror, sign an agreement, and issue them a cashier's check.

Beware of franchisors who ask for a check during Discovery Day. And beware of any franchisor who requests a fee up front to attend a Discovery Day.

Signs You Are Working with a High-Road or Low-Road Franchisor

Low-Road Franchisors	High-Road Franchisors
They appear slick, scripted, rehearsed, and fake.	They appear approachable and genuine. Whether or not they appear formal or informal is part of their culture, but you should be left trusting the feedback you receive.
After shaking hands, you notice your watch is no longer on your wrist.	They already own watches, paid for by the royalty collections generated by scores of successful franchisees.
After meeting them, you have the indescribable experience of being "sleazed" and needing to take a shower.	After meeting them, you have the experience they are telling it like it is in order to give you a realistic idea of the challenges ahead and how they will support you.
If after attending Discovery Day you decide not to join them, they try to make you feel stupid or like you did something wrong.	If you decide not to join them, they will probe into your reasons why. If your decision is based on inaccurate information, they will challenge you. If your decision is based on accurate information, they will support you.
They will apply high pressure sales tactics to force a "yes" decision.	They will hold you accountable for making a final "yes" or "no" decision, but they will not apply undue pressure.
You don't get the opportunity to ask the franchisor's decision makers hard questions. If you do, they tap dance around them or pretend your questions are not relevant.	You get ample opportunity to ask the franchisor's decision makers hard questions. They answer you truthfully.

Low-Road Franchisors	High-Road Franchisors
They try to prove how successful they are by wearing expensive suits and jewelry, expensive haircuts, and having expensive office furniture and an impressive conference room, which appears incongruent with what they appear to be able to afford after reviewing their financials in their UFOC.	They appear to have nothing to prove. They offer you an accurate picture of who they are, without pretense or bells and whistles. Their office furnishings and surroundings are consistent with their financial means.

Franchise Cultures

Another thing you will want to pay attention to is the franchisor's corporate culture, which may or may not reflect the franchisees' culture in the field. The franchisor's culture will fall into a range, anywhere from anarchy to a dictatorship and everything in between. We will spell these out for you.

Keep in mind franchisors are typically private companies. Presidents and CEOs are free to run their companies any way they see fit and you aren't going to change them. Take famed basketball coach Bobby Knight, for instance. Not every collegiate basketball player can play for such a volatile and sometimes demeaning coach like Knight. For others, Knight's style will bring out productivity. Just know who you're doing business with and what you can expect from them moving forward. If you can't play for the coach, find another coach you can play for.

In this section you will learn how to identify the different franchise cultures and what you can expect from each one.

Anarchy

What to Look For: Chaos

What to Expect Moving Forward: More chaos

Franchisors operating inside of anarchy have lost control of their brand and are missing in action. Their franchisees do not value and thus ignore standardization. The franchisor is not enforcing quality standards. The CEO and leadership team have completely lost their ability to lead their franchisees, and franchisees are ignoring their directives. When the franchisor provides little leadership, franchisees create their own systems, processes, quality control, product or service mix, and eventually destroy the value of the brand, which is dependent on uniform and consistent delivery of the product or service. This is a house divided amongst itself. This franchisor and most of their franchisees will more than likely fail, swallowed up by more skilled and better organized competition.

Empowered Leadership

What to Look For: Teamwork and community

What to Expect Moving Forward: Unity and growth

Franchisees and employees of the franchisor are clear about what their roles and responsibilities are. Each is empowered with the authority and resources to get their job done. When there are problems, franchisees and franchisors work together to identify and resolve issues, taking into consideration everyone's needs. Franchisor employees are empowered to make decisions within their realm of responsibility. The franchisor is clear and realizes it needs successful franchisees in order to win and grow their brand. They are committed to listening to the needs of their franchisees and provide or invent tools and programs franchisees can use to produce outstanding results.

Franchisors using an empowered and participatory leadership style will have their egos in check and don't feel the need to always be right. They know their core competencies and where they are weak, and they aren't afraid to request help and support from the franchisee community. Where appropriate, they solicit franchisees' feedback and implement their ideas. Instead of feeling threatened and engaging in a constant power struggle, the franchisors and franchisees believe they are playing for the same team. Franchisees see the franchisor not as a boss or the police, but as a partner in their success. While franchisees may not agree with everything the franchisor is doing, they believe the franchisor is acting in their combined best interest, shows sound judgment, and is fair and equitable in their dealings with the franchisee community.

These franchisors understand and respect that their executive decisions may have a far-reaching impact on the franchisees, franchisees' employees, and their respective families. They also understand that some decisions are best made by the franchisees, with or without the franchisor's input. These franchisors possess the skills and abilities to accurately place decisions in one of four boxes:

1. Franchisor decisions with no input from franchisees
   Examples include who the franchisor hires, what to pay the franchisor's executives and support staff, how to maintain the integrity of the brand.
2. Franchisor decisions with input from franchisees
   Examples would include new product launches and training programs.
3. Franchisee decisions with input from the franchisor
   Examples include trying new advertising vehicles. While it's the franchisees' expense and ultimately their decision, the franchisor will want to know how the franchisee is promoting the brand. The franchisor possesses a reasonable right to reject the vehicle if the brand isn't being properly used.
4. Franchisee decisions with no input from the franchisor
   Examples include who to hire on the franchisee level and what to pay employees. While the franchisor may have guidelines, ultimately this is a franchisee's decision and they don't have to consult with the franchisor.

Management by Committee

What to Look For: Leaders who are in over their heads, always looking to please, afraid of not being appreciated, afraid to make strong decisions, and masquerading as empowered leaders.

What to Expect Moving Forward: Short-term thinking, compromises, and committee decisions meant to appease or please franchisees rather than long-term strategic executive decisions meant to add to their value proposition, strengthen their system, and build the brand.

Franchisors are like any other company. In order to win, a franchisor needs a strong, visionary leader who can create a clear vision of the future, communicate this vision to franchisees and staff, and enroll them in the idea that the vision is a worthy pursuit. These strong leaders need to understand that if others don't buy into their corporate vision *and make it their personal vision*, their vision will not occur. These strong leaders invite participation to the extent they get buy-in. They aren't threatened by feedback. They will incorporate some of their franchisees' and employees' advice into their decision. When rejecting their advice, the strong leader will still give employees and franchisees the experience of being heard and appreciated.

There is an old joke that asks, "What's a camel?" The punch line is: "A horse designed by a committee." While there is nothing wrong with camels, you wouldn't enter one into the Kentucky Derby. Corporate pleasing and compromising pretending to be participatory management is dangerous. Once a leader goes down the tunnel of people-pleasing, they cease to be a leader. They have taken their eye off the bigger prize, which is building a lasting company, strengthening their systems, and building the brand.

This style of management occurs frequently in young franchise systems which sell franchises before they have their systems and processes battle-tested and proven. Franchisees in the course of their day-to-day operations continually identify holes in the franchisor's systems and are forced to plug them. These plugs are often incorporated into the system, meaning you now have franchisees designing the system. In isolated incidences this may be fine, but if it becomes a pattern, the franchisor loses credibility and the ability to lead.

This style of management also occurs in very mature chains with mature franchisees and with franchisors who do not own corporate units. The franchisees who have mastered the KASH formula of success and operate from Winning or the Zone, may have the experience of knowing more than the franchisor. Because they are experts and on the firing line every day, they often do know more. They may see the franchise support staff as "wet behind the ears" or, in the case of franchisors who don't own corporate units, as out of touch and theoretically running the business from the ivory tower instead of from in the trenches. Many times these franchisees are right. If the franchisees have become masters and are being supported by a franchisor who has neither kept up with their industry nor with the skill level of their franchisees, there can be a tremendous loss of credibility and diminished ability to lead. The franchisor may then begin to bow to the demands of aggressive and vocal franchisees, often weakening the chain in the process. The franchise system further breaks down from there and the chain loses momentum.

Benevolent Dictatorship

What to Look For: A charismatic, authoritarian CEO

What to Expect Moving Forward: Whatever the CEO wants

Franchisors operating a benevolent dictatorship don't come out and say, "Hey, we have a peaceful, benevolent dictatorship and it's the franchisees' job to pay homage to the king." They usually pretend to operate from an empowered leadership style, and probably believe they do. Upon a closer look, you'll see disempowered senior-level and midlevel managers whose responsibility it is to carry out the CEO's executive orders. It is one man's company and everyone knows it. In the process of this man winning, others (including franchisees) come along for the ride and win too. This brings with it a sense of community, a kind of "village" feel.

Investing in a benevolent dictatorship is not necessarily a bad thing. Benevolent dictators are often strong, charismatic, and capable leaders with clear vision and great integrity and business ethics. They are often influential communicators, clearly articulating what the vision is to the franchisor and franchisee community and enrolling them in this vision. Often it takes a benevolent dictator to kick-start a franchise to get it going. Once it's going however, this same leadership style may hurt the franchise's forward momentum.

Benevolent dictators frequently do not surround themselves with other strong leaders because they don't want their decisions challenged. They want everyone to know who's in charge. Strong, capable leaders want a forum to express their ideas, so they don't last long while working for a benevolent dictator. The benevolent dictatorship operates under a reverse natural selection process, where only the weak survive. Weak "yes men" managers who execute the benevolent dictator's bidding without question, are mislabeled loyal and team players and promoted beyond their level of competency. Capable senior managers who challenge the logic and opinions of the benevolent dictator are mislabeled troublemakers and rebels, and eventually either resign or are fired. The benevolent dictator may not consciously be doing anything wrong, as they are indeed benevolent. Often the benevolent dictator's family members are called on to fill executive roles, not because they are qualified, but because they are family and the benevolent dictator feels family can be trusted. Trust is more important than competency. But as the chain grows, the lack of competent senior leadership becomes apparent and impacts the performance of the entire organization.

There's also a fascinating paradox which is often operating behind the scenes. Benevolent dictators are often very entrepreneurial. Frequently they are the founder of the franchise and the inventor of the brand. Consider for a second why people start businesses or franchises. The person starting a business usually has had some negative experience with Corporate America, to the point of rejecting the notion of ever working for another company again. The benevolent dictator was likely such a person. However, the franchisor's growth demands that the benevolent dictator create what he or she despises, a corporation. Entrepreneurs naturally resist this organizational transformation often to the point of killing off growth. They want to stay in charge and keep their fingers on the pulse of the business. They want it to be their business, and resist letting the corporation create an identity of its own. They resist this transformation and maintain control by surrounding themselves with weaker players. Because the senior leadership is weak, and the benevolent dictator resists hiring and turning over control he or she is called on to do more and more. Soon the demands exceed what one person is capable of doing. Eventually growth and weak senior leadership can cause severe organizational breakdowns. The benevolent dictator usually responds in one of four ways:

1. Nothing changes. The forward momentum slows or halts and the company eventually settles into something the benevolent dictator and his or her weak management team can control.

2. The benevolent dictator has an "ah hah!" moment and sees himself or herself as the one who ultimately created the organizational breakdown. They also see that their leadership style will not propel the company forward. This new insight opens the door to a personal leadership transformation. They either bring in outside assistance to train and develop leaders or dismiss or reassign weak leaders, and bring in new, strong, and experienced executive leadership. They empower these new leaders to drive the organization forward. They solicit their opinions and implement their ideas. The organization trans-

forms from a benevolent dictatorship into an empowered leadership organization, driven by the personal transformation of the benevolent dictator. Employees, who aren't used to thinking for themselves, will either adapt to these new changes or find another benevolent dictator to work for and continue sleepwalking through their career.

3. They get frustrated and sell their company to professional businesspeople who take the company to the next level, or not.
4. They get frustrated and turn their company over to family members who may or may not be capable of running it.

You as a prospective franchise owner must take into consideration the worst case scenario, which is: "What happens to the franchise system if the benevolent dictator is disabled?"

Dictatorships (Minus the "Benevolent" Part)

What to Look For: A domineering, ego-driven, and frightened CEO, afraid of losing control, pretending to be a strong, visionary leader and disempowered, robotic employees living in fear of losing their jobs pretending they like what they are doing and who they are doing it for.

What to Expect Moving Forward: Intimidation. Command and control techniques. Spying.

The actions of dictators aren't determined by what's right and wrong, but by what they can get away with. Their decisions seem to be designed to control the minds and actions of their franchisees. They are like an overbearing parent who seldom offers praise and is always ready to pounce on problems and mistakes. They have little regard for the franchisees' skills, hard work, and personal investments, and may send franchisees default notices for minor, irrelevant infractions. The CEO's persona can be summarized in two words: no integrity.

In the movie *Broadcast News*, Albert Brooks, who plays the character Aaron Altman, described the devil this way, "What do you think the devil is going to look like if he's around? Nobody is going to be taken in if he has a long, red, pointy tail ... He will be attractive ... He will be nice and helpful ... He will never do an evil thing ... He will just bit by little bit lower our standards where they are important ... flash over substance."

How Brooks will identify and not be taken in by the devil is also how you will identify and not be taken in by a dictator franchisor.

If you spot a dictator, don't necessarily turn and run; figure out whether or not you are in a benevolent dictatorship or a dictatorship minus the benevolence. Both will appear nice and helpful, incapable of doing an evil thing. However, only one will appear genuine. The other is hiding a red, pointy tail.

How to Prepare for Discovery Day

- Get plenty of rest. This will be an exhausting day.
- Know who you are going to meet and what they are responsible for.
- Know what you are going to ask each person. Come with a prepared list of questions.
- Be prepared to answer personal questions. Remember, interviewing for a franchise is not like interviewing for a job. Franchisors can ask you anything. You may hear questions such as, "Have you ever been fired? Have you ever been arrested? What does your spouse think about you wanting to buy this franchise? How much money will you need to borrow?"

How to Successfully Participate in Discovery Day

- Be yourself. Show them exactly who you are and who you are not.
- Ask your questions. No question should be left unasked.
- Pay attention to your surroundings. If you are the type of person who is distracted by taking notes, don't take notes. Instead, pay attention to every conversation and what's going on around you.
- Walk around. The franchisor may confine you to a conference room because they don't want you to see everything. Ask to be shown around the building. If not, walk around the building during a break time. Watch what the employees are doing. Pay attention to the looks on their faces. Are they organized or cluttered? Happy or frustrated? Concentrating or goofing off? Don't ask permission because you might hear, "no." It's better to just walk around, get chastised, and apologize for it

later than to ask permission and hear "no." And no sane, competent franchisor is going to disqualify a franchise candidate because they are curious about what's going on.

Post Discovery Day Evaluation

- Organize your data.
- Consider not making any decisions for at least three days. Just hang out with the information you gathered.

Let yourself be afraid or excited, but don't be duped by your emotions. Being excited doesn't mean this is the right franchise for you, nor does being afraid mean it's wrong. What does your data say?

Decision-Making Checklist

The Big Questions: If you answer any of these questions with a "no," end your investigation and communicate your decision to the franchisor.	Yes/No
Will the franchise opportunity produce my "must have" and "wish to have" objectives with a high degree of probability?	
Do I closely match the franchisor's profile of a successful franchisee?	
Are the other franchisees winning?	
Are the franchisees and franchisors committed to each other's success?	
Does the franchisor know how to give away the KASH formula of the business and accelerate franchisees from the Launch to Winning or the Zone within a reasonable time frame?	
Are the franchisor's advertising and marketing programs effective?	
Will the franchisor give me the proper direction I need to get started?	

The Big Questions: If you answer any of these questions with a "no," end your investigation and communicate your decision to the franchisor. (Continued from previous page)	Yes/No
Am I willing to accept complete responsibility for how my life and business turn out?	
If I invest in this franchise, will I enjoy going to work in the morning?	
Is this a "high-road" franchisor?	

Other Questions: If you answer any of these questions with a "no," do not immediately dismiss the opportunity. Ask "What's missing?" and "Can I live without this?" or "How do I provide what's missing?"	Yes/No
Questions from Chapter 1	
Has the franchisor done a good job bringing in high-quality franchisees?	
Has the franchise sales representative treated me with honesty and integrity? Do I trust their feedback?	
Was the franchise recruiter making an effort to help me determine whether or not I fit their profile of a successful franchisee?	
Will the franchisor do what it takes to help me win?	
Will I do what it takes to win?	
Questions from Chapter 2	
Knowing what they know now, would most of the franchisees make the same decision again?	
Am I willing to leave the path of 99% and take the path of the 1%?	
Am I willing to ignore the taunts of my inner critic and chase my dreams?	
Am I willing to do what it takes to make this business "the right business"?	
Am I willing to do what it takes to make this time "the right time" to start a business?	

Six-Step Franchise Investigation Process

Questions from Chapter 3	
Have I identified my primary behavior style (Action Hero, Comedian, Faithful Sidekick, or Private Eye)?	
Does my "value in business" match the profile of a successful franchisee?	
Does my "ideal franchise" match the franchise opportunity I'm considering investing in?	
Am I willing to work with the franchisor to guard against "what will kill me if I'm not careful?"	
Does the franchisor's support team have the skills, time, and knowledge to help me guard against "what will kill me if I'm not careful"?	
Questions from Chapter 4	
Do I have S.M.A.R.T. goals?	
Do I trust that the franchisor's support people will take on my goals as their goals?	
Am I willing to chunk my goals down into a daily action plan and work this plan every day?	
Have I identified the high-priority activities that generate the most results?	
Am I willing to guard my time wisely and spend most of my time engaged in the high-priority activities that generate most of the results?	
Have I identified the activities that suck time and generate few results?	
Am I willing to not engage in these activities?	
Am I willing to go home every night with the experience of "it's not all finished" and "there's still something left to do"?	
Questions from Chapter 5	
Am I confident I have clearly identified the franchisor's KASH model of success?	

Questions from Chapter 5 (continued)	
Does the franchisor have a strong track record of imparting their KASH formula to the other franchisees?	
Am I willing to do what it takes to acquire the necessary KASH?	
Is the franchisor willing to do what it takes to impart the necessary KASH?	
Questions from Chapter 6	
Do I fully understand what may occur in the Launch, the Grind, Winning, the Zone, and the Goodbye stages?	
Do I accept responsibility to do what it takes to move through the Grind and into Winning and the Zone?	
Does the franchisor have a track record of effectively supporting franchisees in the Grind, and helping them move forward into Winning?	
Question from Chapter 7	
Am I willing to do what it takes to maintain positive, interdependent relationships with the franchisor and other franchisees?	
Questions from Chapter 9	
Do I understand and agree to the terms of the franchise agreement?	
Do I understand and accept the financial risk?	
Do I have the necessary capital to move forward?	
Do I have the necessary financing to move forward?	
Am I clear about what my territory is and do I believe the territory is viable?	
Will I allow the franchisor's leadership to lead me?	

Step Six: Making an Investment Decision

If you have diligently followed this or a franchisor's similar process, you've done an outstanding job of taking a close look at what it takes to win as a franchisee. While you will experience intense emotions such as fear, anxiety, excitement, and possibly anger, this is normal and will be short-lived. Once you've made a decision, you will experience relief.

Thoroughly absorb and evaluate the information in your decision-making worksheet. Prepare to make a decision.

Many people at this stage of the decision-making process allow emotions to corrupt their data. If you want to say "no," you'll have a tendency to dismiss your research, which validates the franchise opportunity and focus on the information which invalidates it. Regardless of the opportunity, you can always find a reason to reject it and miss out on a tremendous opportunity in the process. Keep in mind, before they were well known, 99 percent of the people investigating McDonald's®, Burger King®, Dunkin Donuts®, and Wendy's® found a reason to invalidate these opportunities.

Back in the '80s, before Subway® took off, franchise candidates used to dismiss the Subway® opportunity by telling the franchisor representatives things such as "No one wants to eat in a bright yellow restaurant! Everyone will get headaches!" They also said, "Why did you name your chain 'Subway'? Have you ever ridden a New York City subway? There is graffiti, junk on the floor, gum on the chairs ... no one will eat in a Subway!" At the time of this writing, the Subway Franchisee's Association reports about one in 20 meals eaten in a restaurant are eaten in a Subway.® On one hand you can say the critics are wrong because Subway® has proven to be a dominant global brand. On the other hand, you can say these critics are right, 19 out of 20 meals aren't being eaten at Subway.® You can make the data mean anything and this is exactly what you will also do. At this stage in your decision-making process, it's hard to take an objective look at your data.

To maintain objectivity you can do one of two things. First, you can pretend you're a business consultant. Your client just paid you to take a look at their research and make a cold, hard recommendation based solely on it. What would you recommend?

Second, you can actually go to a business consultant and ask them to make a cold, hard recommendation based on your research. Either way, don't prolong the agony and don't give the franchisor the idea that you're a person who can't decide.

Before you make your final decision, let's explore the four different types of decisions you can make. Whatever decision you do make however, it's our goal that your decision brings you peace.

The Two "No" Decisions

Your research says "yes" but your emotions say "no."

You may discount and dismiss your high probability of winning because you lack confidence in your own abilities and are afraid of losing. Your inner critic is hurling loud, nasty accusations against you and on some level you believe he's right. Not wanting to make a fear-induced decision, you'll create normal and reasonable reasons to say "no." This decision is perfectly valid and will bring you peace *as long as you are honest with yourself.* Say to yourself, "I choose to say 'no,' not because there is anything wrong with the business or because the business is wrong for me. I choose to say 'no' because it's my choice and this is what I chose. I don't need to pretend or to make up a reason."

The Private Eye and Faithful Sidekick behavior styles (from Chapter 4) are most prone to make this type of decision.

Your research says "no" and your emotions say "no."

You have done the work and your research clearly supports a "no" decision. Perhaps you see that you have a low probability of achieving your "must have" and "wish to have" objectives. Maybe you are undercapitalized. Perhaps the concept is not proven and the risk outweighs the reward. Maybe you aren't an organizational culture fit or you don't have confidence in the leadership. Whatever the reason, it's valid. The responsible decision is "no."

Any behavior style is capable of making responsible, data-based decisions.

The Two "Yes" Decisions

Your research says "no" but your emotions say "yes."

This is a recipe for a possible disaster because you bought into hype without substance. You blinded yourself to possible warning signs because you really connected on a deep emotional level with this business. You are confident you can make it work, but perhaps you've ignored evidence that the system doesn't work or that you won't have all the tools necessary to win. This doesn't mean you'll fail. It does mean however, that you've chosen a crooked path to success.

The Action Hero and Comedian are most prone to make this type of decision.

Your research says "yes" and your emotions say "yes."

You have done your homework, put your emotions in check, taken a cold, hard look at the data, and the data makes a compelling case for you to move forward. You match the profile of a successful franchisee and people like you are winning by your definition of winning. And, of course, you are pumped! While this franchise may not be the perfect business, you're going in with your eyes wide open because you've conducted a responsible investigation. You know what it takes to win and you've accepted the responsibility to do what it takes. You have contemplated the risks and determined that the reward outweighs the risk. You have considered your downside, and although losing won't be pretty, you are clear you will survive and rebuild.

Any behavior style is capable of making responsible "yes" decisions.

Now that you know what your four available options are, we offer you our *last* worksheet to help simplify your decision.

Final Decision Worksheet

Please read the following instructions carefully.

Instructions:

Check only one box.

I decide:

Yes ☐

No ☐

Communicate your decision to the franchisor representative. Experience peace, freedom, and joy, and go create a great life and career.

Your process is now complete.

Congratulations.

Conclusion

When we wrote *Street Smart Franchising*, we had you in mind. We tried to anticipate every thought you would have, every emotion you would experience, and every action you would take as you investigate, start up, and run a franchise. We tried to help you uncover and dispel all your myths and misinformation about franchising, including ones you didn't even know you had. We intended to help you create a clean mental space where you could learn what it takes to win in franchising.

Since franchisors report that 99 percent of people who investigate their franchise do not move forward, we started with the premise that left to your own resources, most likely you will not move forward with a franchise. It wasn't because you wouldn't win. Odds were you would throw in the towel before you even tried. By throwing in the towel, you might have passed on an outstanding opportunity that an outstanding franchisor presented to you, missing a chance to design a life and career of your choosing.

While an incredible number of throw-in-the-towel decisions are bad decisions, not all are. Neither are all "go forward" decisions good decisions. Our goal in writing this book was to help you discover and decide what to do with the towel, backed up by facts and information, without being emotionally hijacked by unfounded fears.

We wanted to help you be clear on how your skills, aptitudes, and character traits play out in business, so you can find a franchise that fits; one that builds on your strengths instead of exposing your weaknesses.

We wanted to dispel two prevailing misperceptions that exist. First, that all franchisors are created equal. Like any group, franchisors possess a range of talent and results. Some franchisors are brilliant and have it all figured out. Given the right franchisee with the right capital, success is almost guaranteed. Their customers are stark raving fans. Their marketing works. They know how to give away the success formula of their business to any potential franchisee seeking to learn their craft.

And while some franchisors may be good at running their own company operations, they may, at the same time, be completely incompetent in the business of franchising. Their systems and business methods are either missing or underdeveloped. Results are spotty. Their franchisees are left to their own resources to try to figure out how to win and in the end some do and some don't. Those who don't are faced with terrible consequences.

In the media, you may hear franchising described as either a distribution model or as a business opportunity. This is another myth we wanted to dispel. We want to further the premise that franchising is a business unto itself. For instance, a franchisor can have a brilliant retail or restaurant chain and, at the same time, be a lousy franchisor. We wanted to raise your level of awareness about who is and isn't competent in the business of franchising. We wanted to show you how to pop open a franchisor's hood and take a critical and discerning look at their economic engine. We detailed every engine part, what it's function is, and what happens to the engine if the part is missing or malfunctioning. Our goal wasn't to make you an educated franchise buyer, but a *franchise connoisseur.*

Lastly, the primary reason we wrote *Street Smart Franchising* was to bring purpose into our own lives by trying to make a difference in your life. Helping you was our dream. We wish you much success.

Index

A

Achievement, behavior styles embracing, 39, 40
Action Hero style, 39–44, 57–58
Actions, winning, 73
Advertising-driven franchises, 53
Advertising requirements in UFOC, 184–185
Anarchic cultures, 209–210
Application forms, 174–177
Appointments, 81, 196
Arbitration, 192
Assignment-of-contract rights, 191
Attainability of goals, 64
Attention, 77–78
Attitude
  in Goodbye stage, 136
  in Grind stage, 116–120
  in Launch stage, 108
  role in success, 88, 89
  in Winning stage, 127–128
  in Zone stage, 131
Attorneys, 181

B

Balance sheets, 194
Bank account numbers, 175
Bankruptcies, 182–183
Behavior styles
  Action Hero, 39–44
  Comedian, 45–48
  conflicting, 55–57
  Faithful Sidekick, 48–51
  identifying in others, 57–58
  overview, 34–39
  Private Eye, 51–54

Ben and Jerry's, 12, 16
Benevolent dictatorships, 213–215
Big Mac, 9
Binding arbitration, 192
Bluntness, 39, 42
Body analogy, 6–7
Boogey Man, 119–120
Brands, 51, 163
Broadcast News, 215
Brokerage account numbers, 175
Brokers, 159–160
Brooks, Albert, 215
Business planning resources, 199–200
Business Plan Pro, 200
Business skills, 96, 102. *See also* Skills
Business stages
  Goodbye, 133–138
  Grind, 111–124
  Launch, 107–111
  overview, 98–100
  recognizing in current franchisees, 196–197
  Winning, 124–130
  Zone, 130–133

C

Calling, franchising as, 5–6
Camping Test, 20
Cash flow statements, 194
Cash on hand disclosures, 194
Celebrities in franchises, 192
Chain method, 8
Challenge as franchisee goal, 7–8
Change, fears of, 25–27
Chief executive officers, 209–210, 213–216

Clock time, 68
Coaching
  in Grind stage, 124
  in sale of business, 138
  training versus, 101–102, 104–105
  when franchisors should use,
    106–107
  in Winning stage, 126, 129–130, 137
  in Zone stage, 133
Comedian behavior style, 45–48,
  57–58
Committee decision making, 211–212
Communication
  Comedian strengths, 45
  during franchisee training, 101–102
  impact of differing behavior styles
    on, 55–57
  as sales skill, 109–110
  skills self-assessment, 96
  winning conversations, 72–73
Communities of franchisees, 19–20
Company outlets, 188–189
Compensation of franchise salespeople, 85–86
Compliance, 35
Conferences, 111
Conflicts
  avoidance behavior, 45, 47
  behavior leading to, 42–43
  from differing styles, 55–57
  in franchisee-franchisor relationship,
    146–148, 192
  resolving, 150–151
Conscious competence, 127
Conscious incompetence, 115
Consensus building, 45
Consistency, 52
Consultants, predatory, 10–11
Consulting
  decreasing dependence on, 129, 133
  in sale of business, 138
  training versus, 101–102, 104
  when franchisors should use,
    106–107
  when to seek, 123
Contracts, listing in UFOC, 194

Control
  behavior styles embracing, 42–43
  dictatorial cultures, 213–216
  as franchisee goal, 7
Conversations, winning, 72–73
Cooperation self-assessment, 94
Copyrights, 189
Corporate cultures, 209–216
Corporate officers, 181–182
Cost containment, 48
Covey, Stephen, 60, 75

D

Daily targets, 66, 121–122
Dale Carnegie, 102
Data analysis, 203–206, 217–223
Data gathering, 166–167, 195–203
Deadlines for goal achievement,
  64–65
Death, awareness of, 69–70
Decision making
  about franchise investment,
    217–223
  Action Hero style, 39–40, 41
  Comedian style, 46, 47
  corporate culture and, 210–212
Deficit analysis (KASH model), 92–96
Deluca, Fred, 11
Desired futures, 31–33, 59–60
Development approaches for fran-
  chisees, 17–19
Dictatorships, 213–216
Diplomacy, 50
Discovery Days
  assessing corporate culture during,
    209–216
  high- versus low-road environ-
    ments, 207–209
  importance of, 206
  preparation and participation in,
    216–217
DISC theory, 34–37
Dispute resolution procedures, 192
Distractions, planning for, 80–82
Distribution, franchising as, 3–4
Dominance, 35

E

Earnings potential, 172–173, 192
Efficiency, 40
80/20 rule, 75–77
E-mail, 81
Emotional balance in Grind stage, 118–119
Emotional decisions, 222
Employees
developing, 126–127, 128–129
fallacies about, 27–28
Empowerment, 124, 210–211
Entrepreneur Magazine, 160
Entrepreneurs, 9, 96, 214
The Entrepreneur's Source, 160
Exclusive vendor relationships, 12–13
Expos, 160
Express Personnel, 12
Extraversion, 39–47, 57–58

F

Failure
assessing franchisor experiences from UFOC, 193–194
costs of, 91–92
false experience of, 116
Faithful Sidekick style, 48–51, 57–58
False hopes, 117–118
Family support, 95
Fear of change, 25–27
Fear of unknown, 50, 53, 173–174
Fee disclosures, 183–185
Fee stage, 144–145
Fighting, problem solving versus, 116–117. *See also* Conflicts
Final decision worksheet, 223
Financial data from current franchisees, 197–200
Financial goals, 8, 60–62
Financial statements, 194
Financing, 9, 187
Five-year goal setting, 60–62
Flexibility goals, 7
Formulas, changing, 125–126
Franchise agreements
elements of, 181–195
honoring, 148, 149

importance of reviewing, 166
limitations of, 179–181
Franchise brokers, 159–160
Franchise Buyer, 160
Franchise E-Factor, 142, 153, 154
Franchisee-franchisor relationship
asking current franchisees about, 200–201
Fee stage, 144–145
franchisors' ability to build, 164
Free stage, 147–149
Glee stage, 142–144
legal obligations and beyond, 179–181
Me stage, 146–147
overview, 140–142
See stage, 149–151
We stage, 151–152
Franchisees
common goals, 7–8
costs of poor performance from, 91–92
defined, 3
definitions of success, 22–23
developing, 17–19
estimated number in U.S., 5
goal setting principles, 60–62
interviewing for franchise investigation, 195–204
listed in UFOC, 193–194
obligations in UFOC, 186–187
peak-performing, 90–91, 100
recruiting, 14–17, 83–87
strong communities of, 19–20
training by, 129, 132
Franchise fees, 12, 99, 183
Franchise investigation process
corporate culture analysis, 209–217
data gathering and analysis, 166–167, 195–206
decision checklists, 217–220
final decisions, 220–223
home office visits, 167, 207–209
initial interviews, 167–174
overview, 164–167
qualification, 174–178
reviewing agreements, 179–195

Index

Franchising
  acceptance versus rejection of, 23–27, 30–31
  as business model, 11–14, 20–21, 224–225
  conceptions of, 3–7
  as extension of personal systems, 37
  locating opportunities, 157–160
  reasons for, 7–11
  "right" businesses and times, 27–29
Franchisors. *See also* Recruiting
  approaches to recruiting, 14–17
  asking current franchisees about, 200–202
  defined, 3
  estimated number in U.S., 5
  evaluating, 163–164
  help during Goodbye stage, 138
  help during Grind stage, 123–124
  help during Winning stage, 129–130
  high-road versus low-road, 8–14
  KASH distribution by, 100–107
  obligations in UFOC, 187–188
  revenue sources, 12–13
  UFOC information about, 181–182
Franchoice, 159
Frankl, Viktor, 141
Frannet, 160
Free stage, 147–149
FTC Guidelines to Buying a Franchise, 180
Future, envisioning and designing, 30–33, 59–60

G

Garbage in, garbage out, 203–204
Gibson, Mel, 148
Glee stage, 142–144
Goals
  breaking down, 65–68
  common to franchisees, 7–8
  required attributes, 63–65
  three- and five-year, 60–62
Golf, 111–112

Goodbye stage, 133–138
Gossip, 149
Grading franchisors, 201–202
Grind stage
  applying KASH model, 115–121
  basic features, 111–115
  current franchisees in, 197
  success strategies, 121–124

H

Habits
  in Goodbye stage, 136–138
  in Grind stage, 121
  in Launch stage, 110
  role in success, 88, 89–90
  in Winning stage, 128
  in Zone stage, 132
Health self-assessment, 95
High-profile people in franchises, 192
High-road franchisors
  advertising requirements, 184–185
  basic features, 8–9, 11–14
  home office visits with, 207, 208–209
  product purchase agreements, 186
Hobbies, 111–112
Home office visits, 167, 206–209
Hope, false, 117–118

I

Ideas from franchisees, 9, 20
Impatience, 43
Implementation, 19, 41
Income potential, 172–173, 192
Independence, asserting, 146–147
Influence, 35
Initial interviews, 165, 167–174
Initial investment disclosure, 185
Inner Critic, 25–27
Instant messaging, 82
Interdependence, 152–153
International Franchise Association, 160, 181
Interruptions, planning for, 80–82
Interviews
  with current franchisees, 195–204

initial discussions with franchisors, 165, 167–174
skills for conducting, 109
Introversion, 48–54, 57–58
Involvement, 41

J
Job fit, 37–38
Jung, Carl, 34–35
Juran, Joseph, 75

K
KASH model of success
applied to Goodbye stage, 135–138
applied to Grind stage, 115–121
applied to Launch stage, 107–110
applied to Winning stage, 127–128
applied to Zone stage, 131–132
basic features, 87–91
franchisor transmission to franchisees, 100–107
matching to franchising opportunities, 162–163
obtaining others' assessment, 96–97
self-assessment for, 92–96
Kenny Rogers' Roasters, 192
Knight, Bobby, 209
Knowledge
in Goodbye stage, 135
in Grind stage, 115–116
implementation versus, 19
in Launch stage, 108
role in success, 88, 89
in Winning stage, 127
in Zone stage, 131
Kroc, Ray, 11

L
Launch stage
applying KASH model, 107–110
current franchisees in, 196–197
success strategies, 110–111
Lawn Doctor, 189
Lawsuits, 91, 180, 182
Leadership
Action Hero approach, 41, 43
dictatorial, 213–216

empowered, 210–211
ineffective, 209–210
self-assessment, 94
Legal reviews of franchise agreements, 166
Listening, behavior styles and, 40, 43, 52
Lists of outlets, 193–194
Litigation section (UFOC), 182
Local advertising requirements, 184
Long-term debt disclosures, 194
Low-road franchisors
basic features, 9–11
home office visits with, 207–209
product purchase agreements, 186

M
Magazines, 160
Management by committee, 211–212
Marketing requirements for franchisors, 163
Marston, William Moulton, 34–35
Mastery, 17–18
McCormack, Mark, 63
Measurability of goals, 63–64
Merle Norman Cosmetics, 12
Me stage, 146–147
Modeling skills, 103
Modification of franchise agreements, 192
Molly Maids, 189
Moral obligations, 182–183
Motivation self-assessment, 94
Multi-tasking
behavior styles challenged by, 49, 53
behavior styles embracing, 41
fallacies about, 77–78

N
Nathan, Greg, 93, 142, 154
National advertising funds, 184–185
Networking, 152
Newspapers, 160
"No" decisions on franchising, 222
Noncompete clauses, 192
Noncurable defaults, 191

Index

O

Objectivity, 49
Obligations to participate, 190
Occupancy costs, 199
Online questionnaires, 168
Operating costs, 199
Opinions, stating, 39–40, 42
Opportunities for franchising, 157–160
Optimism, 47, 117–118

P

Pain as progress, 113–114
Pareto principle, 75–76
Participation obligations, 190
Patents, 189
Peak-performing franchisees, 90–91, 100
Perfectionism, 53
Performance/satisfaction curve, 99
Persistence, 49
Personal challenge, 7–8
Personal finances, answering questions about, 170, 175
Personal information on application forms, 174–176
Personal questions during interviews, 169, 216
Personal responsibility self-assessment, 95
Personal systems, 37
Pessimism, 118
Peters, Tom, 80
Plans, disturbing, 80
Poor performance, costs of, 91–92
Practice, 102, 121
Private Eye style, 51–54, 57–58
Problem solving, 41, 45, 109
Procedures
    assessing ability to comply with, 95
    behavior styles embracing, 49
    behavior styles resisting, 42–43, 46
Product restrictions, disclosing in UFOC, 186
Product sales, importance to franchisors, 12–13
Profitability, 179–180, 197–200

Proprietary information, 189
Protected territories, 188
Public figures in franchises, 192

Q

Qualification, in franchise investigation, 165–166, 174–178
Quality
    behavior styles embracing, 52, 53–54
    in franchise recruiting, 86–87
Quality of life goals, 60–62
Questionnaires, 168

R

Rating franchisors, 201–202
Realistic timetables for goal achievement, 64–65
Real time, 68, 69–82
Rebates, 186
Receipt of UFOC, 194
Recruiting. *See also* Franchise investigation process
    Discovery Days, 206–209
    measurement tools for, 35–36
    media for, 158–160
    requirements for franchisors, 163
    sales representatives for, 83–87
    for top-quality franchisees, 14–17
Relationships, franchising as, 4, 140–142. *See also* Franchisee-franchisor relationship
Remedial training programs, 101
Renewal fees, 185
Renewal terms, 190
Restricted sales, 190
Results orientation, 39, 40
Results/satisfaction curve, 99
"Right" businesses and times, 27–29, 79–80
Risks
    behavior styles avoiding, 48, 50
    behavior styles embracing, 41, 43, 46
    choosing to live with, 71
    as excuses for rejecting franchising, 23–24, 25–27

fallacies about, 27–29
reducing by franchising, 9
from Winning stage, 132
Rita's Water Ice, 12
Royalties
disclosing in UFOC, 184
dissatisfaction with, 144–145
maximizing, 13–14
from peak performers, 90
relative importance to franchisors, 12, 13, 100

S
Sales of businesses, 137–138
Sales representatives (franchisor)
Discovery Day pitches, 207–209
initial interviews with, 165, 167–174
priorities and abilities, 83–87, 206
take-aways by, 178
Sales restrictions, disclosing in UFOC, 190
Sales skills
Comedian strengths, 46
in communication, 109–110
self-assessment, 94
Sandler, David, 103
Sandler Sales Institute, 102, 103
Satisfaction of current franchisees, 200
See stage, 149–151
Skills. *See also* Training
business versus technical, 102
in Goodbye stage, 136
in Grind stage, 120–121
in Launch stage, 108–109
modeling during training, 103
relation to behavior styles, 55
role in success, 88, 89
in Winning stage, 128
in Zone stage, 132
Small business resources, 199–200
S.M.A.R.T. goals, 63–67
Snipe hunts, 29
Social Security numbers, 175
Solitude, preference for, 52
Specialization, behavior styles favoring, 54
Specificity of goals, 63

Sport Clips, 190
Stages. *See* Business stages
Starbucks, 188
Steadiness, 35
Structure
behavior styles avoiding, 46
behavior styles embracing, 49, 52
Subway restaurants, 11, 154, 221
Success. *See also* KASH model of success
defining, 22–23
goal achievement principles, 65–67
goal setting principles, 60–65
job fit and, 37–38
KASH model features, 87–91
real-time truths, 69–82
Survival thinking, 122
Systems orientation, 95, 161–162

T
Take-aways, 178
Team development, 126–127, 128–129
Technical knockouts, 134
Technical skills, business skills versus, 102
Telephone calls, scheduling time for, 81
Tempers, 43
Termination rights, 190–191
Territories, 188–189
Thoughts, winning, 72
Three-year goal setting, 60–62
Time management, 67–68, 96
Time, real versus clock, 68, 69–82
Timetables, realistic, 64–65
Timing, fallacies about, 28–29, 79–80
To-do lists, 74
Total occupancy costs, 199
Total owner benefit, 198
Trademarks, 189
Training
asking current franchisees about, 197
assessing ability to receive, 93
challenges for franchisors, 18–19
decreasing dependence on, 129
by franchisees, 129, 132

Training (*continued*)
  franchisor approaches, 101–103
  as ongoing process, 110–111, 123
  requirements for franchisors, 163
  in sale of business, 138
  when to use, 106–107
Transfer fees, 185, 191
Transfer-of-franchise terms, 190, 191

U

Unacceptable futures, 32–33
Unconscious competence, 17–18
Unconscious incompetence, 109
Undercapitalization, 170
Uniform Franchise Offering Circular
  (UFOC)
  earnings information in, 172–173
  elements of, 181–195
  importance of reviewing, 166
USA Today, 160

V

Vision, 40, 45, 60

W

Wall Street Journal, 160
Wasted time, 75–76, 81
Wealth goals, 8

Web sites
  franchise brokers, 159–160
  *FTC Guidelines to Buying a
    Franchise*, 180
  International Franchise
    Association, 181
  listing franchising opportunities,
    157–158
  small business resources, 199–200
We stage, 151–152
Winning stage
  applying KASH model, 127–128
  overview, 124–127
  risks in, 132
  success strategies, 128–130
Win-win solutions, 149
Working capital, 185
Work-life balance, 7
Wright, Steven, 115
Written goals, 63

Y

"Yes" decisions on franchising,
  222–223

Z

Ziglar, Zig, 59
Zone stage, 130–133